THIS INCREDIBLE LAND

AN INFORMAL GUIDE TO THE HISTORY OF SOUTH AFRICA

WENDY WATSON

Second edition published 2015 by
David Philip Publishers (Pty) Ltd
6 Spin Street, Cape Town 8001

First edition published 2007 by New Africa Books (Pty) Ltd

ISBN: 978-1-4856-2284-0
epub ISBN: 978-1-4856-2303-8
emobi ISBN: 978-1-4856-2304-5

Editing by Jane Argall
Layout and design by Fresh Identity/Peter Stuckey
Illustrations by Fresh Identity
Proofreading by Ingrid Brink
Cover design by Nick Mulgrew

Printed and bound by Creda Communications

*David Philip is committed to a sustainable future for our business,
our readers and our planet.*

CONTENTS

FOREWORD BY ARCHBISHOP DESMOND TUTU

It is now more than 10 years since the Truth and Reconciliation Commission began its work.

The Minister of Justice, the late Mr Dullah Omar said, in his introduction to the commission: "... *a commission is a necessary exercise to enable South Africans to come to terms with their past on a morally accepted basis and to advance the cause of reconciliation*".

This book gives us an opportunity to examine the long history which led up to the human rights abuses which occurred in South Africa, and to exult in the demise of apartheid. It is written on a dateline, giving details of significant events from pre-history until 2004 – 10 years into the democratic dispensation. It does not analyse, and merely states facts as they occurred, enabling the reader to draw their own conclusions.

A statement from a survivor of the war in the Natal Midlands stated, at his hearing in Pietermaritzburg in November 1996:

"*Even though I haven't mentioned this in my statement they came on a Thursday, that is on the 29th. They got there and they killed a woman who had just given birth. They also killed the newborn baby. Even the elderly people who could not run away were killed. It was quite a terrible situation. It was like something from a horror movie*".

How do individuals and communities recover from such wounds?

So often people thought that theirs was the only community to suffer. Because of the disinformation campaign, many people failed to understand the full context of the suppression. The public hearings of the Truth and Reconciliation Commission changed these perceptions and gave people the opportunity to see the entire picture. Remembering the pain and suffering expressed at the TRC enables one to see the miracle of the new South Africa, which is almost beyond comprehension.

There is a sign at the Apartheid Museum in southern Johannesburg which reads: "Apartheid is finally where it belongs – in the Apartheid Museum".

There have been miraculous changes in the country, which has developed a proud Constitution that guarantees human rights, and assists us to find areas of compromise and reconciliation in our "Rainbow Nation".

As we grow in our efforts at reconciliation, may we work towards a future free of discrimination and pain. And may this book add to our knowledge base so that we can continue the work of rebuilding a free and fair society, and continue the miracle.

Archbishop Emeritus Desmond Mpilo Tutu

Past Chairperson of the Truth and Reconciliation Commission

Nobel Laureate

May 2006

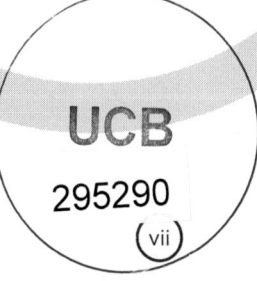

AUTHOR'S NOTE

There is a Zulu saying which goes: "*The history of hunting will always be told from the perspective of the hunter, until the hunted write their own history*". As a white South African woman, am I a hunter or the hunted? History has many perspectives and this book, although it tries to be impartial, will have its own.

The writing of this book has been somewhat self-indulgent. Because of having worked in the Truth and Reconciliation Commission, many people ask me about our recent history, mainly the political dimensions, and show an amazing lack of knowledge and understanding of our past. Even more people have misconceptions about what ACTUALLY happened in South Africa – even those events which occurred during their lifetimes. The 'disinformation' campaign of the previous regime was very successful in maintaining ignorance of the realities of both the colonialist and apartheid eras.

I am not a historian, nor a politician, or a professional writer, but have felt for some years that a concise layman's history of South Africa would be a useful document for most homes. What actually happened? What truths or lies were we taught at school or by our parents? What led to our mainly peaceful transition in 1994? Why are we experiencing the societal problems that we have today?

The motivation to write *Brick by Brick* came after a visit to the Apartheid Museum in Johannesburg, where I found no suitable book that reflected history in a concise way in the bookshop. The time came during a period of recuperation from cancer and chemotherapy in 2002.

Many people choose not to read detailed analyses of political events, so I have put together a short, simple, and I hope accurate, history of South Africa. This is in no way a comprehensive history, but touches on issues which I consider to have had far-reaching effects on our country. For convenience and reference purposes all the information has been placed against a timeline.

One of the challenges in writing a book about a country whose policies were based on race classification is how to refer to the various races. I have tried to use 'black' and 'white' wherever possible, but have also sometimes used European, African, Native and Bantu where I think it gives an indication of the historical perspective of the time. Similarly, language and cultural issues determine the usage of words denoting ethnic classification. I must apologise if I have offended anybody by my choice of labels.

Another challenge was not to project my own memories and story within the struggle in the main text of the book. My first awareness of apartheid was being put off the train, with my brother and 'coloured' nanny as we were all in the same carriage, going to the beach. We had to move into the 'second class' compartment where she was able to travel. I must have been about four at the time. I remember her fury. The second memory is of the 1956 men's march, when we were stuck amidst the marching men on de Waal Drive, when I was about eight. I do not remember being afraid. I only remember being amidst the thousands of men, marching solemnly into the city to protest about carrying passes. Most of them were dressed in grey suits and hats. I remember my mother explaining to me the significance of the Womens' Day March also, and the referendum in 1960 which led us into a republic and away from the Commonwealth family.

In my adult life there are lots of incidences – leaving South Africa in 1971 to live in England after a demonstration in which my mother was arrested; being involved in trying to stop demolition of shacks in informal settlements in the late 1970s and 1980s; and having hundreds of people living in tents and caravans within our church garden when they were left without homes after such action.

In 1994 I was involved in forensic investigations of state violence, some of which led to the conviction and punishment of those involved. Then the management of an organisation collecting written materials prior to the Truth and Reconciliation Commission (TRC). The TRC experience would make a book on its own, and it was a privilege to be part of the process. It was difficult and life changing for everybody involved. Obviously for those who came to testify as victims/survivors, and those amnesty applicants involved in the human rights violations, the memories that were brought back were extremely painful.

Maybe my own memories belong in a document for my children, and as a process of reflection for myself.

The story of South Africa, particularly our joint memories, should be recorded as a lesson for the future. My own part in the transition process was infinitesimal. I was not a role player, or even really a participant in change on a macro scale. There has been so much pain and suffering of so many over the centuries, what right have we, as privileged whites, to claim to have suffered? But in reality everyone in South Africa has suffered through the social engineering, commonly called apartheid. We carry the burden of exploitation of many developing countries with the same results in terms of the environment, the economy and the social issues which have arisen as a result of colonialisation. This book does not intend to analyse those issues.

The daily reminders that we see on the streets are the legacy of colonisation and apartheid – the lack of adequate health care and housing, poor education, the extremes of poverty and wealth, the materialistic vision of many South Africans, and of course the violence, crime and lawlessness which so pervades our society today and appears to be an expression of anger of even those who were too young to directly suffer suppression.

I must acknowledge the contribution made by Jane Argall who took my concept and very rough draft, and has edited, researched, rewritten and generally brought the story to life, producing a far better analysis than my hasty scribblings. Jane has spun silk from straw, and I cannot thank her enough. Jane has her own history in the struggle and was also part of the TRC process as a researcher and editor. She made time to do this work while involved in her own projects, including one with young people in prisons, and I am eternally grateful to her for her attention to detail, and her willingness to pick up the pieces that I had left out, and to cut out extraneous issues which did not add to the story.

My thanks go also to my daughters, Sarah and Mary-Ruth, who have given me the time and space to move into very challenging areas in my work. Sarah also had a hand in the editing and added a politically sensitive touch to my dated concepts. Mary-Ruth compiled the index which improves access to the book when memory for dates is sketchy. My life-partner, Olive Douglas, has given me unconditional love and encouragement in my work for more than 15 years, and also supported the writing of *Brick by Brick*.

Sincere thanks too to Archbishop Desmond Tutu for writing the forward to the book, and to Advocate Dumisa Ntsebeza for the 'shout' for the cover. They are two of the real heroes of the struggle.

I sincerely hope that you enjoy dipping into this book from time to time, as much as Jane and I have enjoyed putting it together.

Wendy Watson

AUTHORS NOTE TO THE REVISED EDITION

Brick by Brick was first published in 2004 in response to the need for a simple account of South Africa's turbulent history. It must again be emphasised that the author has not analysed or commented on the history in this book – it is merely a timeline stating what happened when, and not necessarily why or how.

This revised edition includes Chapter 12 dealing with the period 2004 to 2014.

It has been extremely difficult to find positive events in the past ten years and I am not alone in that conclusion. Followers of columns by Max du Preez, Eusebius Mc Kaiser, Mondli Makhanya and others will also have found their musings verging on the negative. The 2014 publication by Alex Boraine, "What's Gone Wrong? On the brink of a failed state" also focuses on the challenges of the last decade rather than the achievements, as do the works of Clem Sunter and others.

We, as South Africans, hoped for so much in our new democracy. So much had been put into the efforts to transition from the colonial and apartheid eras into a new dispensation. There is no doubt that strides have been made in regard to various issues of human rights, and progress to undo the harmful events of the past. But there is still so much to do, with the issues far more difficult to identify and counter.

These are the bare bones of the last decade of the story – the analysis and judgement is up to you, the reader.

The Last Century at a Glance

Public Protector report on corruption in the Nkandla construction was published.	2014	National and Provincial elections. ANC gained 62% majority, DA 22% and EFF 6.35%.
Economic Freedom Fighters formed.	2013	5 December. Death of former President Nelson Mandela, at age 92.
Nearly 40 people die (2 police, 34 protesters) in the Marikana Massacre.	2012	Julium Malema suspended then expelled from the ANC.
SA Becomes part of the BRIC grouping of countries.	2011	
FIFA Soccer World Cup in SA.	2010	
Construction begins on security upgrades at Nkandla	2009	Zuma suspended as deputy President. but subsequently elected as President in the General Elections.
The power supply from ESKOM begins to collapse and "load shedding" begins.	2008	Mbeki resigns and Kgalema Motlanthe takes over as president until the next elections.
Jacob Zuma succeeds Thabo Mbeki as presidential candidate.	2007	
Same-sec marriage legalised in SA	2006	Gauteng Freeway Project construction begins (e-tolling system)
Zimbabwe elections won by President Mugabe. Validity still under dispute	2005	US supports AIDS relief with large scale ARV program
Celebrations to mark 10 years of democracy. ANC won 70% of votes in general election.	2004	Announcement, SA to host FIFA 2010 World Cup Soccer tournament.
Charlize Theron won an Oscar.	2003	
Further land grabs in Zimbabwe – seizure of white-owned farms. SA team summited Everest.	2002	Mark Shuttleworth joined the Russian space team and visited the International Space Station.
43 people killed in stampede at soccer stadium.	2001	
R50 billion arms deal agreement. Devastating floods in Mozambique.	2000	International AIDS conference in Durban.
Landslide victory for the ANC in general election.	1999	Thabo Mbeki inaugurated as President.
President Nelson Mandela married Graça Machel.	1998	SA invades Lesotho to quell army mutiny while President Mandela overseas.
New Constitution finally adopted by Parliament.	1997	Value of the Rand tumbled from R8 to the US$ to around R20.

SA participated in the Olympic Games for the first time since 1960. Human Rights Commission established.	1996	National Party withdrew from government of national unity and moved into opposition. Minister of Finance unveiled GEAR policy.
Truth and Reconciliation Commission established. Compulsory schooling introduced for all children from 5 – 14.	1995	Bafana Bafana won the Africa National soccer cup. Springboks won the Rugby World Cup.
First democratic election. New flag designed and adopted.	1994	Revolts in Bophuthatswana and Ciskei. Clashes between IFP and ANC at Shell House. Sabotage campaign by right wing.
Transitional Executive Council (TEC) came into being – to ensure elections free and fair. Nelson Mandela and FW de Klerk awarded the Nobel Peace Prize.	1993	Oliver Tambo died.
Release of more political prisoners. International Commission of Jurists visited SA. Referendum (for whites only) to determine support for CODESA process. 70% voted for further reforms.	1992	Chris Hani assassinated. Bisho massacre – 30 died. Boipatong Massacre: 40 died and 27 seriously injured.
Nadine Gordimer won Nobel Prize for literature. Convention for a Democratic South Africa (CODESA) – forum to negotiate new constitution. First black judge appointed to the bench.	1991	National Peace Accord signed. Black children admitted to previously white schools for the first time. Repeal of Population Registration Act. Release of political prisoners. First group of exiles returns to SA. Countries lifted sanctions against SA.
2 February: de Klerk announced sweeping changes and unbanning of political parties. 11 February: Nelson Mandela released. Namibia became independent. 14 killed and hundreds injured by police in Sebokeng.	1990	Groote Schuur minute – agreement on conditions for negotiations. Repeal of some discriminatory legislation. SA Comunist party re-established. Oliver Tambo and Thabo Mbeki returned to SA after years in exile.
David Webster murdered. FW de Klerk took over from PW Botha as President after the latter had a stroke.	1989	Harare Declaration – policy for negotiated political settlement. Soviet Union disintegrated. Launch of the defiance campaign.
Stanza Bopape died in detention. Riots in Bophuthatswana, quelled from SADF. Restriction orders on Cosatu and the United Democratic Front.	1988	State sponsored acts on individuals continued. Trust Feeds massacre. Barend Strydom killed six people and injured 16 in a massacre in Pretoria. 166 cases of AIDS reported.

Govan Mbeki released, placed under restriction orders. Albie Sachs injured in car bomb explosion in Maputo. Other activists killed and injured.	1987	Midlands War in KZN between ANC and IFP. Operation Vula launched by the ANC.
Guguletu Seven shot dead in Cape Town. SADF attacked Zambia, Zimbabwe and Botswana. Economy in state of crisis. Increase of economic sanctions against SA.	1986	Various SA groups (including George Bizos) visited ANC in exile. Eminent Persons Group visited SA for talks with Mandela and others. Bomb outside Magoos Bar in Durban beachfront.
Nine people killed by police during 'free Mandela' march on Pollsmoor prison. Death toll 28 by end of week. Victoria Mxenge murdered. Killings by police in Uitenhage, Cape and other areas. Four members of PEBCO killed by police. UDF/Inkatha conflict escalated. PW Botha Rubicon speech.	1985	Four UDF activists abducted and killed in Cradock, Eastern Cape. State of Emergency declared. COSATU launched. Lawlessness in townships. Explosion in shopping centre in Amanzimtoti. MK operative Zondo executed later. UDF campaign to make townships ungovernable.
Nkomati Accord signed. Clampdown on media.	1984	Bishop Desmond Tutu awarded Nobel Peace Prize.
Tricameral parliament came into being. Continued detentions of activists. Pretoria bomb. 21 killed, over 200 injured.	1983	Protests and riots throughout the country. UDF launched.
Conservative Party formed. Many activists died in detention.	1982	London offices of ANC bombed. Cross border raid into Lesotho – 42 killed.
Attack on ANC activists in Mozambique. 20 killed. Some prison reform – political prisoners moved from Robben Island to Pollsmoor.	1981	
	1980	Student activists killed. Rhodesia gained independence, and became Zimbabwe. School boycotts resulting in exodus of youth to ANC in exile.
Relationship between Inkatha and ANC deteriorated. State Security Council formed. Legalisation of African trade unions.	1979	Some aspects of 'petty apartheid' removed. Venda granted independence.
SANDF killed over 600 at Kassinga in Angola.	1978	

Bophuthatswana and KwaZulu-Natal offered independence. Military conscription increased to two years.	1977	Winnie Mandela banished to Brandfort, Free State. Banning orders on 17 anti-apartheid organisations.
Political unrest in townships leading to Soweto uprising – against Afrikaans in schools.	1976	First television broadcasts. Transkei given independence.
Mozambique and Angola gained independence from Portugal.	1975	Chief Buthelezi revived Inkatha.
Parcel bomb killed activist in Botswana. Letter bomb killed activist in Zambia.	1974	Metal and Allied Workers Union established.
	1973	Wave of strikes.
Schlebush Commission investigated several NGOs and curtained their work.	1972	AWB formed – right-wing Afrikaners. Black People's Convention formed.
ANC consultative conference in Tanzania.	1969	South African Students Organisation formed. International sports sanctions.
Dr Chris Barnard performed first heart transplant. Liberal party disbanded. Military service introduced for white males.	1967	Bureau of State Security formed. Nearly a million people arrested in this single year. Coloured Persons Representative Council formed.
SA troops clashed with SWAPO at start of 23 year long war in Namibia.	1966	Verwoerd assassinated by Dimitri Tsafendas.
Ian Smith declared UDI in Rhodesia. 90 day detention doubled.	1965	Bram Fischer and others arrested.
Bomb detonated in Johannesburg Airport by John Harris of the radical white African Resistance Movement.	1964	
Rivonia trial of activists. Mandela and others imprisoned.	1963	
Deaths in detention.	1962	Emerging underground resistance and increasing suppression.
90 day detention law introduced. Nationalists won general election. SA becomes independent republic.	1961	Chief Albert Luthuli won Nobel Peace Prize and banned.
Sharpeville Massacre. 69 protesters killed. Macmillan 'Winds of Change' speech. Referendum among white South Africans – about becoming a republic.	1960	
Eight 'Bantustans' came into being.	1959	Pan African Congress formed. Riots in Durban (Mkhumbane) by women.

Hendrik Verwoerd assumed leadership.	1958	
SA National anthem adopted.	1957	Bus and tax boycotts.
Tomlinson Commission recommended changes to reserves. Sophiatown razed, and replaced by white suburb named Triomf. Senate Act removed coloured males from voters role.	1956	20 000 women marched to Union Buildings to protest passes. "You have struck a rock". 156 Congress leaders arrested for treason – for publishing the Freedom Charter. Start of 5 year long Treason Trial.
Freedom Charter adopted by ANC and alliances.	1955	SA Congress of Trade Unions formed. Black Sash formed.
Federation of SA Women formed.	1954	Alan Paton published *Cry the Beloved Country.*
Separate Amenities Act. Bantu Education Act.	1953	Liberal Party of SA formed.
Legislation to ensure carrying of passes enacted.	1952	Defiance Campaign – 8 000 arrested.
Suppression of Communism Act. Censorship became active.	1951	Bantu Authorities Act.
Population Registration Act and Immorality Amendment Act introduced.	1950	Increase in acts of civil disobedience.
	1949	ANC adopted plan of action – stepping up civil disobedience.
Implementation and entrenchment of Apartheid.	1948	National Party comes to power.
	1947	Congress Alliance bringing together Natal Indian Congress and ANC.
100 000 strong strike by AMWU. 12 shot dead by security forces.	1946	Indian Passive Resistance Campaign launched.
End of Second World War.	1945	
	1944	ANC Youth League formed by Nelson Mandela, Walter Sisulu, Oliver Tambo and others.
United Party (1934) won the general election.	1943	Formation of ANC Womens' League.
Non-European Unity movement formed.	1940	Dr Alfred Xuma became president of the ANC.
Outbreak of Second World War.	1939	
Centenary of Great Trek celebrated by formation of Ossewabrandwag.	1938	
African voters disenfranchised.	1936	Land allocation to reserves doubled.

Broederbond backed new fusion party.	1934	United Party formed under Hertzog as Prime Minister.
SA left the gold standard.	1932	
White women given the vote.	1930	
Wall Street crash – great depression.	1929	Federasie van Afrikaans Kultuurverenigings (FAK) formed.
Sex between racial groups became illegal.	1927	
Legislation to prevent blacks from forming trade unions, but allowed other groups.	1926	
Afrikaans replaced Dutch as official language.	1925	Plethora of legislation to entrench white rule.
Pact government furthered segregationist policies.	1924	New flag replaced Union Jack.
Native Urban Areas Act passed – entrenching pass system. Land ownership by blacks prevented.	1923	52 killed in the Bondelswarts protest in Namibia.
White mine workers strike. Marshall law declared.	1922	214 strikers killed.
Bulhoek massacre. 183 killed by state forces	1921	African Independent Church Movement started.
	1920	
General Jan Smuts became Prime Minister.	1919	70 000 African miners went on strike. Troops broke up meetings and killed 11.
End of World War 1.	1918	ICU formed by dock workers.
	1917	First African trade union formed. (Industrial Workers of Africa).
Outbreak of World War 1.	1914	National Party formed under Hertzog.
Natives Land Act passed. 13% of land for blacks, 87% for whites. Mahatma Gandhi led protest march.	1913	Mines protests. 800 women arrested after protest against pass laws.
Afrikaaner Nationalist Party formed under General Hertzog. Dedicated to racial separation and republicanism.	1912	SA Native Congress formed. Later (1923) to become ANC.
Mines and Works Act made it difficult for black workers to obtain skilled work.	1911	
Four states merged to form Union of SA. General Louis Botha became Prime Minister, introduced policy of racial segregation.	1910	

South Africa Act passed in Britain – power given to white minority.	1909	African Political Organisation formed.
National Convention entrenches white supremacy under unitary state.	1908	African delegation to London to protest – ignored.
Chinese labourers repatriated.	1907	Publication of *Jock of the Bushveld*.
Poll tax introduced. Attempts to reconcile English and Boer populations.	1906	Bambatha uprising. 3 000 black men and 30 white men killed at Nkandla in Natal.
Denial of black civil rights increases.	1905	
Indentured Chinese labourers imported to work on mines.	1904	
SA Native Affairs Commission formed.	1903	Pass system introduced.

CHAPTER 1

EARLY DAYS

5 million BCE to 1500 ACE

Most scholars agree that Africa is the probable cradle of humankind. We begin by touching on what appears to be the earliest signs of life on the sub-continent.

For generations South African children were taught that the history of the country began in 1652 with Jan van Riebeeck landing in the Cape to set up a refreshment station for ships travelling to and from the east. In fact there is a wealth of pre-colonial history in the southern African region – written and oral, true and fable – which puts the Van Riebeeck story into a different kind of perspective.

More than 2,5 million years ago

The earliest forms of pre-human existence (australopithecines or southern apemen) have been traced to the southern African sub-continent. Fossilised australopithecine evidence was found in the Sterkfontein valley outside Johannesburg. The Sterkfontein cave system – known now as the **'Cradle of Humankind'** – was proclaimed a World Heritage Site in 1999.

Less than 2,5 million years ago

Australopithecus evolved into the 'family of man' (hominidae).

Scientists differ on the **origins of modern humans**. While some believe that the modern human emerged between 40 000 and 50 000 years ago, another school holds that modern humans evolved over a longer period going back as far as 250 000 years.

THE QUEST FOR HUMAN ORIGINS

A revolutionary advance in the hunt for human origins came with the 1925 discovery of a skull at Taung by the esteemed palaeontologist, Professor Raymond Dart. In subsequent decades many hundreds of hominid fossil specimens have been found in excavations at the Sterkfontein and Kromdraai cave systems near Johannesburg.

According to a contemporary palaeontologist, Professor P V Tobias, two distinct kinds of hominid lived in Africa around a million years ago, namely *Homo Erectus* and *Australopithecus*.

In 1998 an entire australopithecine skull and skeleton was found at Sterkfontein and is estimated to be between 3,2 and 3,5 million years old. The *Australopithecus* became extinct while *Homo Erectus* maintained its presence in Southern Africa, although it is not known when exactly these hominids arrived or became extinct. It would appear that *Homo Sapiens* evolved directly from *Homo Erectus* with the transition taking place 1,5 to 1,6 million years ago.

Less than 2,5 million years ago

Evidence of stone tool-making in Africa marks the beginning of the **Earlier Stone Age.** Some of these tools were excavated at the Sterkfontein and Swartkrans sites in Gauteng and at Elandsfontein in the Western Cape.

Less than 250 000 years ago

Refinements in tool-making saw the production of hand-axes and cleavers in what is described as the **Middle Stone Age**. Artefacts suggest that those who made them applied sophisticated thought to the design and honing of such items. It is believed that this cognitive ability links middle and later Stone Age people with their modern San descendants.

Increasingly hunter-gatherer Stone Age people were using caves and rocks for shelter. From this era, archaeologists have found burial sites and stone engravings indicating that people were capable of abstract thought and may have engaged in ceremonial practice. There is also evidence that fire may have been used in the cultivation of food resources. Domestic hearths which have been excavated suggest that people formed family or kinship groups.

Less than 120 000 years ago

Evidence gathered in the **Tsitsikamma** coastal areas of the Western Cape, and at **Border Cave** in northern KwaZulu-Natal indicates that anatomically modern humans were present in these areas.

THE STRANDLOPERS

The strandlopers (literally: 'beach walkers') were shellfish-eating hunter-gatherer people who lived a mobile existence in small bands throughout the sub-continent's coastal regions. Middens found on the coasts and in coastal caves in the southern and western Cape suggest that the strandlopers used shellfish as a food resource from about 120 000 years ago. In midden heaps dating back to the later Stone Age, the remains of birds and animals have been found, as well as artefacts made from shells. These important finds have enabled archaeologists to construct a picture of the lifestyle of early strand-lopers, their migration patterns and environmental conditions.

A fossilised footprint of a woman found in the Langebaan area of the Western Cape was dated back to around 117 000 years ago. Dubbed 'Eve's footprint', it is one of the earliest human fossils found in the world. The woman is presumed to have been a strandloper.

Less than 22 000 years ago

The **Later Stone Age** is marked by further refinements in stone tool-making, with the introduction of blades, knives and arrowheads. Rock paintings in cave shelters, still evident today in many parts of southern Africa, have revealed more concrete evidence of lifestyle and cultural practice. Evidence of human habitation in this area is found principally in the more fertile coastal areas where people cultivated food resources and harvested shellfish from the sea. At Noordkappers Point on the Cape coast near Still Bay, stone barriers were built in the tidal shallows for trapping fish. Some of these sea traps are still in use today.

5000 BCE

Domestic animals were present in Egypt and the Sahara around 5000 BCE. It is likely that migrants moved with their livestock down the east coast of Africa over the next 3 000 years.

1000 BCE

San peoples in the northern reaches of present-day Botswana acquired domesticated livestock and began to move south.

THE SAN

The hunter-gatherer San people could be described as the true indigenous inhabitants of southern Africa in that their genetic origins can be traced to the emergence of modern humans in the Later Stone Age. They became widely dispersed across the sub-continent and banded together in small kinship groups that varied with changing climatic and environmental conditions.

San culture and belief systems were closely attuned to the natural environment. This is particularly evident in surviving cave and rock art. Using powdered pigments, the San frequently depicted scenes from the natural world which illustrated how closely their lives were entwined with it.

Their traditional way of life was significantly affected by their contact with African migrant agro-pastoralists and Khoi herders. To some extent San groups integrated with these groups. Historians have attributed, for example, the presence of click sounds in Bantu languages to the intermingling of African and San communities.

It was not until much later – with the arrival of the European colonists – that San peoples were threatened with extinction. Faced with the pressures placed on them by competing groups, San peoples had to choose either to resist change through a defence of their territories and traditions, or to assimilate into a more powerful order. Those who managed to resist incorporation found themselves pushed to the remote areas of what is today Botswana and Namibia. The surviving San communities in these areas remain the only genuine San peoples in southern Africa today.

Beginning of Christian Era

African Iron Age communities were spreading southwards from the northern and eastern regions of Africa.

EARLY AFRICAN MIGRANTS

By the time of the birth of Christ 2 000 years ago, there is evidence that African migrant farmers, speaking early dialects of Sotho, Pedi and Tswana, were moving south from the northern and eastern regions of Africa, bringing sheep with them. Some came to settle in the eastern parts of South Africa, speaking Xhosa and Zulu dialects. Early African migrant communities made and used pottery. Their crops included sorghum, millet, legumes, the African groundnut, and various gourds and pumpkins. Gradually, these migrant mixed farmers spread more widely across the territory.

At around this time the nomadic **Khoi** (also known as the Khoen Khoen) peoples migrated to the south-western parts of the 'Cape'.

THE KHOI

Believed to have originated in the Great Lakes region, the Khoi (Khoen Khoen) people migrated in nomadic groups to the Zambezi valley in east Africa 2 000 years ago. As they came up against other African Iron Age and San groups in competition for access to water, grazing and food resources, they migrated southwest towards the Okavango swamps, southwards towards the Vaal and Orange Rivers, and further east towards the eastern Cape coast. From here, groups spread along the southern Cape coast towards the peninsula and further west towards Saldanha Bay.

The Khoi people were herders and relied on pastoral activities for their survival. They moved regularly to renew grazing pastures and lived in portable dome-shaped huts covered with grass mats. Similarly constructed mat houses ('matjieshuise') are still used by Nama-speaking descendents of the Khoi today.

Archaeological evidence found at the Boomplaas cave near Oudtshoorn shows that the cave was occupied first by San hunter-gatherers (>2 000 years ago) and by Khoi groups from 1 700 years ago. The Khoi used the cave as both a shelter and a stock pen. Pottery shards excavated from the site revealed that the Khoi moulded vessels in distinctive shapes and with pouring spouts.

Some have called the conflict over land use between San and Khoi the earliest expression of racial tension in South Africa. The 'Khoi-Khoi' saw themselves, as herders, as superior to the hunter-gatherer Khoi-San. Nevertheless, during this period there was some degree of assimilation and intermingling between the San hunter-gatherers and the Khoi herders. As a result, it became difficult to distinguish between the 'Khoi-San' and the 'Khoi-Khoi'.

200 – 300 AD

African Iron Age communities were established in what later became known as the Transvaal and Natal (Limpopo, Mpumulanga and KwaZulu-Natal). These communities consisted of Bantu-speaking peoples who had moved down from central and east central Africa.

IRON-WORKING MIGRANTS

These communities could make metal objects which meant they mined minerals and had access to fire. People lived in settled villages, grew crops, kept livestock and were engaged in crafts such as pottery. Pottery shards found in the Lydenburg area reveal the development of new forms of clay-working at this time. Ecologists and historians have suggested that the extensive use of wood by these communities, for building, cooking and smelting, drastically altered the ecology of the region, which changed from savanna to grassland. Communities were generally small but in larger settlements would be organised into chiefdoms, with chiefs deriving their status from the number of head of cattle they owned. In other words, wealth and heredity became an instrument of political power and social control in these communities. These patriarchal communities developed a belief system based firmly in ancestral worship. Ancestral spirits were believed to control natural phenomena like rain and drought and to influence every aspect of life. Misfortune therefore could be dealt with by ritual and ceremony aimed at appeasing the ancestors.

500 – 900 AD

Iron Age settlements in Limpopo, Mpumalanga and KwaZulu-Natal were similar, with each village enjoying political and economic independence. There is evidence of trade in ivory and glass beads, probably from India, dating from this period.

MAPUNGUBWE AND GREAT ZIMBABWE

Archaeological finds suggest that the Mapungubwe state, in the central Limpopo River Valley, was established in the 11th century and, at its height, was the largest kingdom in the African sub-continent. As a powerful state it traded gold through the East African ports with both Arabia and India.

In the 1930s a golden rhinoceros excavated from a grave in Mapungubwe Hill showed that the Iron Age inhabitants of the area were able to mine and work with gold long before the 'discovery of gold' by Europeans in the 19th century.

The Mapungubwe nation state was abandoned after 400 years in the 14th century. The kingdom of Great Zimbabwe, an offshoot of Mapungubwe dating back to the 15th and 16th centuries, was established by Shona-speaking people further north in what is today Zimbabwe. At its height Great Zimbabwe was a thriving economic power in the region. Under apartheid education, children were often erroneously taught that the Great Zimbabwe was remains of an ancient city-state built by the Phoenicians.

Today the impressive stone remains of both the Mapungubwe settlement and Great Zimbabwe are almost untouched. Historians have described these two sites as the cradle of modern day civilisation in the SADC region.

1300 – 1500

The southern African interior came to be populated by **Sotho-** and **Tswana-speaking peoples** in the northern territories and by **Nguni speakers** in the south-eastern and coastal areas. The San had by this time become fairly established in the south-western regions.

During this period various **European seafarers**, mainly from Portugal, Holland and England, explored a sea-route around the south coast of Africa.

1460

Portuguese navigators put ashore at points along the coasts of west Africa, mainly with the purpose of procuring 'slaves' for the European slave market.

1485

The first Portuguese seafarers landed near Walvis Bay in the search for a navigable route around the Cape to the east. Navigation around the southern tip of Africa was treacherous.

THE FIRST EUROPEANS

In 1489 Portuguese explorer Bartolomeu Dias was the first European to sail around the tip of Africa in a quest to open a navigable passage to the trading markets of the east. Skirting around the Agulhas current, he landed at Mossel Bay and later at Algoa Bay (near Port Elizabeth) where he erected a stone pillar. A mutiny by his seafarers then caused him to turn back to Portugal. On his return voyage, he sighted what is now Cape Town and named it Cabo de Todos los Tormentos ('The Cape of all Storms'). Believing that a passage to the Indies had been opened, it was renamed Cabo de Bõa Esperanza ('The Cape of Good Hope').

Eight years later another Portuguese explorer, Vasco da Gama, set out also with the intention of opening a sea passage from Europe to the east. He was successful in securing the Cape of Good Hope as a stop-off and trading station en route to India. Continuing up the east coast of southern Africa, da Gama sighted the KwaZulu-Natal coast and named it Terra do Natal ('Land of Birth') as it was Christmas time.

The Portuguese, as well as other European fleets, continued to use the Cape as a 'pantry' – to refresh and re-stock for ongoing voyages to the east. An island in Saldanha Bay and another off Cape Town (now Robben Island) were used for the purpose. Saldanha Bay was a regular port of call as it had rich sources of food in birds, birds' eggs and other animals as well as a sheltered natural harbour. The main reason that Cape Town on Table Bay was eventually settled was for its access to fresh water running off the Table Mountain, although this was much later.

Minimal contact was made by the visitors with the indigenous population. Such interaction as existed did little to dispel the lack of understanding, ignorance and fear experienced by the various cultures.

1500

Other European seafaring nations began to use the Cape route to India. The Portuguese bypassed the Cape station after the Viceroy of Portuguese India, Francisco d'Almeida, was killed in a clash with Khoi Khoi in Table Bay. The English navigator, James Lancaster, established rather more successful trading relationships with the local Khoi-Khoi people.

CHAPTER 2

SETTLEMENT AND COLONISATION

1600 – 1900

After about 150 years of rather random calls at the Cape by passing seafarers from many European nations, the Dutch eventually sent a contingent to settle there, to provide a source of fresh food for passing ships by growing crops and trading for livestock with the local Khoi people. This would address the problem of scurvy which so severely afflicted the sailors.

It was a period when the Dutch and English made every effort to stop French colonisation of the region, and custodianship of the Cape passed between these two countries several times.

Nearly 200 years passed before a permanent harbour was built in Table Bay in 1860 (the Alfred Basin) and another 80 before the present Duncan Dock was constructed after reclamation of the foreshore in the mid 1900s.

CHAPTER 3
THE 17TH CENTURY

1647

Following the foundering of the Dutch vessel, the **Nieuwe Haerlem**, in Table Bay, surviving crew members camped at the Cape until they were relieved and returned to Holland a year later. On returning to Holland, one Leendert Janszen recommended the establishment of a Dutch refreshment station at the Cape. In his report he said that the castaways had been well treated by the Khoi people with whom they came into contact. He recommended that in setting up a fort at the Cape the settlers should repay the Khoi people's kindness and should honourably enter into bartering and trade with the Khoi so as to build relationships free of mutual fear and suspicion.

1652

Dutch seafarer **Jan van Riebeeck** (1619 – 1677) landed at the Cape with three small ships, the Dromedaris, the Goede Hoop and the Reiger. On behalf of the **Dutch East India Company** (the Vereenigde Ooste-Indische Compaigne/VOC) based in Batavia[1], he established a settlement to re-fresh and re-stock ships sailing to the east. Within the first few years of his ten-year stay at the Cape, he raised a fine vegetable garden to supply visiting ships with fresh greenstuffs. The Company Gardens in the centre of Cape Town remain a historical focal point today.

ROBBEN ISLAND

During Van Riebeeck's time, a few convicts were also sent to the Cape outpost. From early on in the history of the European settlement at the Cape, Robben Island was used as a place of detention and banishment. In the 20th century it was used for some time as a mental asylum, a leper colony and as a naval base. Over centuries many ships have foundered in

[1] The VOC was headquartered at Batavia, a Dutch enclave in Indonesia where Jakarta stands today. The name 'Batavia' refers to the 'Batavi' people who inhabited Holland in Roman times.

stormy seas and on rocks around the island, leaving a litter of wrecks and an abundance of phantoms and maritime ghost stories. Perhaps the most famous of these is of the *Flying Dutchman*, a phantom vessel which appeared in ghostly apparition to seamen in the 18th and 19th centuries. Today Robben Island is famous for the prison which held Nelson Mandela and many other political prisoners for many years during apartheid rule.

1655

Van Riebeeck deployed several individuals to explore the potential for farming and trading in the local interior. From the earliest time of European settlements at the Cape, tensions developed between the settlers – as they probed further into the interior – and the local Khoi-San communities, principally over land and grazing rights.

1657

Five years after the original settlement was established, the immigrant population of the Cape settlement had increased to 130 people. The VOC encouraged more European people to settle at the Cape to stimulate the economy, and granted land rights outside the settlement boundaries to a few individual settlers, known as **'free burghers'** (vryburghers), to raise crops to help meet the demand of passing ships for fresh produce. Local Khoi-San communities were severely affected by the increasing encroachment of the burghers onto their land.

SLAVERY

From the early beginnings of the colony a cheap and reliable source of menial labour was needed. The VOC had regularly imported slaves to various parts of the Dutch empire and in 1657 sent the first slaves to Cape Town. The slaves, who originated from east African and south-east Asian countries had no rights whatsoever and they were subjected to humiliating and brutal treatment by their owners. Many deserted although not always successfully. They were generally not paid, working for food and shelter only, and regularly 'rewarded' for their labours with a tot of alcohol. The tot system (known in the Cape as the 'dop system') eventually produced a massive and longstanding problem of alcohol abuse in descendent slave communities. In 1807 – 150 years later – the Abolition of the Slave Trade Act was promulgated in Britain. This banned trading in slaves but not slave ownership. It was another 27 years before slavery was finally abolished in 1834.

1658

On Van Riebeeck's request, the VOC reluctantly approved the import of **slaves** to the station in 1658. The slaves were set to work in the gardens and on farm projects for the refreshment station. In the first five years of the Cape settlement, Van Riebeeck – forbidden by the VOC to enslave the local population – had relied on the ad hoc depositing of stowaway slaves by passing ships. The first of these slaves 'given' to Van Riebeeck in this fashion was a man known as 'Abraham'.

EARLY GUERRILLA WARFARE: THE KHOI-SAN AND THE SETTLERS

The cattle-herding Khoi people, settled north-east of the Hottentots-Hollands mountains, had in some respects a mutually profitable relationship with the European settlers, and often bartered their wares for metal goods, tobacco and alcohol. However the vast majority of newcomers observed no formalities and showed no respect for the indigenous communities of the Cape, and resentment among the Khoi-San grew.

When they were denied access to pasture or suffered theft of their livestock, the Khoi-San would carry out isolated arson attacks on settler crops and homesteads. In reprisal burghers in commando units launched several armed attacks on the Khoi-San. In 1677 the VOC administration signed treaties with certain chiefdoms, in effect co-opting their support against other communities. This tactic was successful in dividing and displacing local communities and ultimately in diffusing any political bargaining power the Khoi-San had in the early colony.

1660

Van Riebeeck ordered the planting of a **wild almond hedge** along the boundaries of the settlement, principally to erect a barrier between the settlers and the local Khoi-San. Parts of the hedge still exist today in Cape Town's Kirstenbosch gardens.

1660

Horses were imported to the Cape from Batavia, facilitating expeditions into the interior and the setting up of trade relations outside the peninsula area. This was the first important advance in 'communications' in the settlement. Outposts of the Cape settlement were established in Hottentots-Holland and Saldanha Bay.

1665

Dominus Johan van Arckel arrived in the Cape bringing with him the seeds of organised **Dutch Reformed** religious practice. Presbyteries were set up in new settlements.

1674

Building on the **Castle at the Cape** was completed. It was used both as a fort and a prison. As a prison, it was referred to as the '*Donckle Gatt*' (donker gat or dark hole) – a place which no ray of light ever penetrated, even on the brightest day.

1679

Simon van der Stel (1639 – 1712) arrived at the Cape where he took up the post of Commander of the Colony. Twelve years later he was elevated to Governor. Van der Stel, of both Dutch and Indian ancestry, would most probably have been classified 'coloured' if he'd arrived in the Cape in the 20th century, and certainly would have been unable to vote, let alone hold office. Under his control in the 17th century, however, the Cape settlement expanded and prospered. What had been a settlement for stocking up on food was now an emerging colony. The magistracy of Stellenbosch, formerly Khoi Khoi land, was introduced. The gardens flourished, becoming an important botanical and horticultural centre. Wine-making techniques developed, and soon Van der Stel himself became an exceedingly wealthy man, famous for the fine wines to emanate from his own handsome estate, Constantia.

1685

Two hundred industrious and upright **Protestant Huguenots**, originating in France, arrived in the Cape also under the auspices of the Dutch VOC having fled from religious persecution. Van der Stel had appealed to the VOC to send people with experience in wine-making. Their addition swelled the size of the colony by a third and contributed to the development of the Cape wine industry. They populated the new towns of Franschhoek and Drakenstein (both previously falling under various Khoi Khoi chiefdoms) and were happy to work the land and to oblige Van der Stel's insistence that they assimilate culturally and linguistically into the Dutch community in the Cape.

1699

Willem Adriaan van der Stel (1664 – 1733) succeeded his father as governor of the colony. History remembers Willem as a self-interested and nepotistic man, committed to enriching himself as his father had done before him. He set up his sons in prosperous farming enterprises and for himself built up the largest estate in the colony – Vergelegen. Protests against the corrupt ways of Willem van der Stel reached the VOC in Batavia and finally resulted in his recall in 1707.

CHAPTER 4

THE 18TH CENTURY

Early 1700s

As the size of the colony increased, there was further movement of burghers outside its boundaries and further incursion into the agricultural and pastoral land of the Khoi-San. With the gradual encroachment of Trekboer bands, strengthened with commando units, they suffered attack, forced removals and enslavement. Surviving communities, such as those later known as the Griqua people, were concentrated north of settler territories.

At the same time some Khoi Khoi and Khoi-San people came into the colony to work as herders or in the towns.

Although there was exploration and movement on the part of the Trekboers away from the central colony, its role as a trading station was paramount. From the 1770s the number of Dutch ships visiting the port declined and foreign ships from Britain, the USA, France and Denmark visited the port in increasing numbers.

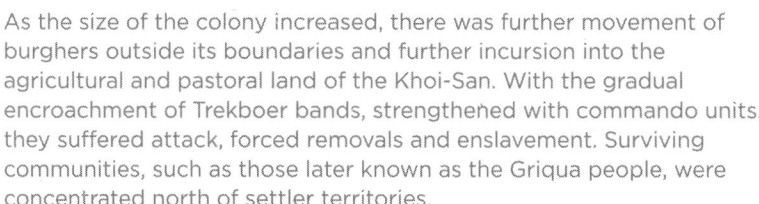

THE TREKBOERS

Dutch migrant farmers or burghers who left the colony precincts in search of a better living in the interior came to be known as Trekkers or Trekboers. In order to secure suitable agricultural land, they dispossessed local indigenous communities of their livestock and access to land. Frequently Khoi-San individuals and families were forced to work on settler farms. As resources became depleted the Trekboers would penetrate further into the interior.

The Trekboers saw themselves as distinct from the settlers in Cape Town. They were hardworking and hardy of spirit. They cultivated a strong sense of group identity based on rigid Calvinist religious beliefs and practice, and on the development of a Dutch dialect which absorbed words from other languages in use at the Cape. This dialect represents the earliest expression of Afrikaans.

It is interesting to note that not all the Trekboers were white. A few freed slaves, Cape coloureds and Africans also made treks into the interior.

With no laws forbidding inter-racial mixing, there were thousands of cross-racial marriages in the Cape in the early days of colonisation. Many slave women were successful in securing their freedom by marrying white settlers. Their offspring were generally recognised as 'white' and they inherited settler surnames.

However, the Cape administration soon passed laws stratifying the colony, with whites (VOC officials and free burghers) in the top strata and slaves and locals in the lower strata. By this time European settlers were referring to the local Khoi-San as 'Hottentots', a term which derisively imitated Khoi-San language.

1713

A **smallpox** epidemic decimated the Khoi-San people (as well as a significant number of colonists) making it possible for colonial farmers to appropriate more land.

1734

The eastern boundary of the colony was extended to the Great Brak River following the VOC's setting up of an administrative post at Rietvlei.

1734

A **Moravian mission** was established for the Khoi-San at Baviaanskloof (now Genadendal). As colonial policy at the time did not make provision for Khoi converts to enjoy equal political and civil status as the colonists, the mission was not a success. With pressure from neighbouring burghers, the mission dissolved and was not replaced for another 60 years.

1745

The districts of **Tulbagh**, north of Cape Town, and **Swellendam**, in the east, were proclaimed as settler farmers moved inland to graze their cattle and grow crops.

THE GRIQUAS

The Griqua people have their biological origins in marriage between the Khoi Khoi people and diverse other groups including settlers and slaves. In this sense the moulding of Griqua identity is a uniquely South African event. Known to the colonial authorities as the 'Basters' or 'Oorlams', the Griqua came into being practising Christianity and speaking the 'taal' – Afrikaans. Under the leadership of Adam Kok I (1710 – 1795), Griqua communities first settled in the Piketberg area of the western Cape. With white farmers exerting increasing pressure on their grazing lands, they gradually moved further north, settling eventually in posts along the Orange River in the northerly parts of the colony.

Succeeding his father, Cornelis Kok (c.1746 – 1820) became chief, settling his chieftaincy at Campbell. He sent his son Adam Kok II (1811 – 1875) to settle at Klaarwater, a missionary settlement later renamed Griquastad. Here Adam Kok and his cousin, Barend Barends (d.1839), were installed as permanent chiefs. They were, however, displaced by the election of Andries Waterboer, a favourite of the missionaries who themselves came to exert considerable influence in the religious and political affairs of Griquastad. In the 1870s when the Griquas, under Nicholas Waterboer (1819 – 1896), laid claim to diamond diggings in Griqua territory, the Cape government proceeded to annex the area known as Griqualand West, on the pretext of 'protecting' the Griquas from the Boers but effectively superseding the Griqua and all small claims to diggings in the area.

With the election of Andries Waterboer, Kok II migrated with his people, settling eventually at Philippolis. In the Philippolis captaincy, however, he was unable to maintain his authority which was gradually eroded by internal divisions among his people, and further the encroachment of white farmers migrating from the south.

Adam Kok III (1811 – 1875) succeeded his father as chief in Philippolis in 1837. In 1842 Kok III negotiated a treaty with the Cape government. The treaty recognised the independence of the Griqua and granted them land ownership, a supply of arms and some measure of protection against further encroachment from the south. The treaty did not last, and succeeding Cape governors reneged on the land agreements, recognising instead the rights of white farmers to half of the Philippolis captaincy.

Griqua autonomy fell by the wayside with the 1848 proclamation of the Orange River sovereignty by the British, and the 1854 establishment of the independent Republic of the Orange Free State. Refusing to cede his captaincy to the Free State government, in 1861 Kok III led his people in a 'great trek' across the Maluti Mountains where they settled in an area known then as Nomansland (later called East Griqualand). Under considerable duress, the Griqua re-built their communities and in 1864 proclaimed 'Kokstad' as their capital.

Ten years later Kokstad was annexed by the Cape government. When Kok III died the following year, his granddaughter's husband Abraham Stockstrom Le Fleur I (1867 - 1941) became chief. A visionary and a prophet, Le Fleur led an epic 40 year campaign to re-unite the Griqua people and re-instate Griqua autonomy.

1750s

Colonial expansion in an easterly direction was slow owing to difficulties of terrain and communications. However, by the 1760s the frontier extended beyond the Gamtoos River into the domain of the amaXhosa, and by the 1780s had spread as far as **Graaff-Reinet** in what is now the Eastern Cape.

During this decade the settlers encountered the amaXhosa who had for centuries been settled beyond the Fish River, which was made a boundary with the Cape in 1771. There were continual skirmishes on the border with cattle being confiscated or stolen by both sides.

1751

Under the governorship of Ryk Tulbagh, the **first library** was set up in the colony as well as a horticultural and zoological collection in the Company gardens.

1770s

Conflict between the Trekboers and the San on the south-western frontiers of the colony intensified as the San were robbed of their traditional territories and as they proved unwilling and unable to be co-opted into a pastoral economy in the colony. Faced with near starvation, the hunter-gatherers engaged in something of a guerrilla war against the colonists, attacking their homesteads and livestock.

GENOCIDE

In what some historians describe as a series of genocidal atrocities, large numbers of San people were killed or captured in VOC-approved commando operations in the south-western Cape. The Trekboer colonists, who could not relate to the San people culturally, socially or racially, were unrestrained in their attempts to annihilate them. For the Trekboers, San men could play no role in a pastoral economy and were deemed to be expendable. San women were sometimes drawn into domestic work and San children used as herders. With the destruction and alienation of San family units the colonists rendered San children open to enslavement simply in order to survive.

It was only after the British occupied the Cape in the 1790s that any attempt was made to restore the peace. However conflict between the San and the colonists in the south-western Cape continued well into the 19th century, decimating the group even further. By the turn of the 20th century the indigenous San culture and way of life was almost extinct and the /Xam language, spoken by the largest San grouping in South Africa, was no longer in use.

Today two San groups still living in South Africa are the !Xû and the Khwe. Many of these people have been settled in the Schmidtsdrift area near Kimberley, having formerly been employed as trackers by the South African Defence Force in its occupation of Namibia and Angola during the years of apartheid.

CONFLICT WITH THE AMAXHOSA

The Nguni-speaking amaXhosa lived in tightly-knit farming communities in the eastern Cape and the 'Transkei'. They put up a formidable defence of their territories against Boer encroachment across the Fish River in the 1770s. Initial skirmishes developed into full-scale warfare. Xhosa commandos responded to sustained Boer attacks on their chiefdoms with counter attacks on settler property and livestock. The VOC could do little to defuse the situation as it lacked the authority for intervention. This lack of effective intervention prompted rebellion against the VOC by a local group of Boers calling themselves the Patriots, who proclaimed for themselves the independent Republic of Graaff-Reinet. The rebellions spread to other areas of the colony and ultimately played a part in ending VOC rule over the Cape.

1782

The **Rix dollar** was introduced as the unit of paper currency in the Cape.
It was used for over 100 years, eventually being replaced by British currency in 1825.

1789

The **French Revolution** had an impact on the colony with the arrival of a French garrison in the Cape to help the Dutch protect their interests in the face of a possible threat from the British. The influx of men into the colony produced a boom in the local economy. It did not last long enough to fully deflect discontent in the burgher population however. Moreover, new ideas developing in Europe and the New World not only increased the tensions in the colony but prepared the ground for a liberal backlash against what had become to be perceived as an authoritarian, corrupt and reactionary VOC government.

THE ARRIVAL OF THE MISSIONARIES

In the 1790s European mission societies began setting up stations in the colony with the re-establishment of the Moravian mission at Baviaanskloof (now Genadendal) near Cape Town in 1792. This was soon followed by missionary settlers from churches in Britain, France, Germany and Holland. The missionary enterprise in South Africa is regarded with some ambivalence today. While many see the planting of Christianity in southern Africa as an attempt to spread European culture and influence by eroding the traditions, culture and social integrity of indigenous peoples, others have argued that the missions championed the rights of the poor and the oppressed in the region and increasingly became involved in political and social advocacy on their behalf – during the early days, in the anti-slavery movement and more recently in the anti-apartheid movement.

1794

The **Auwal Masiid mosque**, the first Islamic place of worship was opened in Cape Town, catering to Islamic slaves from east Asia.

1795

A **British** fleet sailed into Table Bay and took over the Dutch Cape Colony with little resistance from the VOC, which by this time severely lacked political legitimacy. Under the new administration, the local economy took a significant turn for the better and by 1797 the British Governor had succeeded in dismantling the rebel republics of Graaff-Reinet and Swellendam.

By the end of the 18th century, the slave **population** stood at 25 000, outnumbering both the 20 000 white burghers, and the 15 000 Khoi-San, as well as the 100 free blacks. Burghers felt insecure and feared rebellion. Mutinous slaves faced severe punishment for any acts of crime or insubordination.

Privileged whites were already putting in place a social and political structure which would ensure their continued domination of society.

1799

Khoi-San 'servants' revolted in the eastern districts of the Cape, leaving their farms and plundering the homes of Europeans in a campaign aimed at seizing lost ancestral lands. This revolt led to the deaths of 29 settlers. It took four years to quell the rebellion before the 'servants' returned to their farms to work for the settlers.

Asked why they were fighting, one of the Khoi-San replied ... *"[to] restore the country of which our forefathers have been despoiled by the Dutch, and we have nothing more to ask"*.

It was a full two centuries before this dream materialised.

FRONTIER WARS

At this time and in a loose alliance with the Khoi rebels, the amaXhosa also launched attacks on Boer properties and were at first successful in driving Boer farmers out of the Graaff-Reinet district. Frontier conflict continued into the 19th century with heavy-handed attempts from both the Xhosa commandos and the now-British colonial militias to secure areas around the Fish and Keiskamma Rivers. The balance of power shifted with victories on each side until 1820 when, in an effort to keep control of the frontier, the British seized the advantage by settling thousands of British immigrants in the Grahamstown area.

In 1835 British troops entered the territory of Xhosa Paramount Chief Hintsa (c.1790 – 1835). He was taken prisoner for allowing his subjects to enter the Cape Colony and steal cattle. He promised to persuade his people to return the cattle, but was taken into custody. When he tried to escape, he was shot by a British soldier, and his body was mutilated by the soldiers. Following this incident, the British annexed the area between the two rivers but were forced to back down by pressure from 'home' and opted instead for concluding treaties with local chiefdoms.

This did not end the frontier wars, however, which continued until the 1850s when in the final three-year war, the amaXhosa were conquered by superior fire power.

CHAPTER 5

THE 19TH CENTURY

The 19th century particularly was a time of constant movement and realignment for the peoples of southern Africa. Though some of these nations were born or consolidated through conflict and warfare with others, many South Africans today express pride in their ethnic roots, their lineages and in the history of suffering and struggle which brought their groups into being at this time.

It was a century in which white settlers continued to seize control of huge areas of the country, denying the indigenous peoples the rights to their land.

This land-grab was formalised in legislation over the next century, culminating in the Natives' Land Act of 1913 and finally the Group Areas Act of 1950 under the Nationalist government. In the mid-1900s the Land Act separated all races by ethnic origins, giving nearly 90% of the land to whites who made up around 12% of the population.

1800

The **amaXhosa** re-settled west of the Fish River having been driven by the Dutch from the same area several times previously.

1802

Famine and drought further north brought upheaval and strife to the Nguni people living in the 'KwaZulu' area.

1803

The **Dutch** once again took control of the Cape. For two years it was run by Lieutenant-General J Janssens.

1805

The **British** occupied the Cape by force, clashing with burgher commandos at Blaauwberg.

SAARTJIE BAARTMAN (1789 – 1816)

Sarah (Saartjie) Baartman – the 'Hottentot Venus', a young Griqua woman, was employed in the early 19th century as a servant to a local farmer in Cape Town when she came to the attention of English surgeon, William Dunlop, because of her extraordinary physical characteristics, including her enlarged buttocks and unusually elongated labia.

Around 1810 Dunlop persuaded her to travel with him to England where he promised she would become rich and famous. In England Baartman was subjected to scientific scrutiny and public exhibition. For four years she was paraded naked around the streets of London as a bestial curiosity. She saw little of the profits from her 'performances' and in 1814 was handed over to a travelling circus in Paris. A comic opera known as 'The Hottentot Venus' was staged in France, dramatising European preoccupation with 'aboriginal aberration'.

To cope with her humiliation, Baartman worked as a prostitute and turned to alcohol until her death on 1 January 1816. After her death her body was dissected and studied, her genitals and brain pickled and displayed at a museum in Paris until they were withdrawn from public display in 1974.

In the early 1990s a campaign for the return of Saartjie Baartman's remains to South Africa gathered momentum. It was not until March 2002, however, that legal action in the French courts enabled the return of her remains. Nearly 200 years after she had left for Europe, her remains were returned to her home country in a box draped with the South African flag. She was laid to rest in August 2002 in her ancestral home at Hankey in the eastern Cape.

1809

Cape governor, the Earl of Caledon, introduced the '**Hottentot Proclamation**' laying down rules for the employment of Khoi-San labour on farms. Effectively this amounted to the introduction of a pass system as it restricted the freedom of the Khoi-San to seek work.

1811

The Earl was succeeded by **Sir John Craddock** who resolved to take a more offensive approach to the amaXhosa on the eastern frontier and sent a British army to reverse gains made by the amaXhosa on the west bank of the Fish River.

1814

The Cape was formally ceded to Britain and **Lord Charles Somerset** arrived to take up the post of governor, a position which he held through many of the border frontier wars which took place over the next few decades.

1820s

English immigration was encouraged in an attempt to stimulate economic growth and diversification in the colony. The Cape government recruited around 5 000 people to make the four-month sea voyage to settle in the new colony. Under Somerset, English became the compulsory language of learning. This move was resisted by Dutch parents, who refused to send their children to the new free English-speaking schools.

An '**English**' **civil service** was also set up, with English becoming the language of government, to the exclusion of Dutch. Protestant churches were also introduced throughout the Cape, breaking the Dutch Reformed Church's dominance of Christian religious practice.

THE 1820 SETTLERS

Arriving in Algoa Bay, many of the immigrants were settled on small farms in the newly created district of Albany on the eastern frontier of the colony. However, the land turned out to be unsuitable for cultivation and with a succession of climatic disasters as well as Xhosa incursions around the Keiskamma and Fish Rivers, the project failed. Many of the immigrants moved towards the Port Elizabeth and Grahamstown areas, building these centres into viable commercial and urbanised towns.

ROBERT MOFFAT (1795 – 1883)

In 1821 Robert Moffat arrived at the Cape and journeyed to the Kuruman mission in the service of the London Missionary Society. He stayed at the mission for 50 years during which he learnt and transcribed Setswana – the language of the Batswana – and translated and printed the first bible in an African language. In his time a great mission church was built, often referred to as the 'Cathedral of the Kalahari'. Timber for the church's roof was supplied by the fugitive Matabele chief Mzilikazi (1789 – 1868) with whom Moffat had a strong relationship. The Moffat homestead, which still stands today, was the earliest settler-built dwelling north of the Orange River.

1820s and 1830s

At this time there was a great deal of movement and political strife in the African communities of southern Africa. The protracted regional wars are known as the '**Mfecane**' (in Nguni) or the '**Difaqane**' (in Sotho and Tswana) – a term translated as 'forced dispersal'. Famine and food shortages forced indigenous communities to migrate, and in the ensuing conflict some communities were displaced further north, some realigned themselves and some were absorbed by others more militarily powerful than their own. By 1825, Boer and Briton settlers had come to refer to the Mfecane as the 'Wars of Calamity'. Over two million vanquished people were homeless and starving, and wandering through the territories in search of respite.

A dominant feature of the Mfecane was the rise of the Zulu nation through expansionism and military conquest.

SHAKA (1785 – 1828)

The son of a minor chief and an unranked woman, Shaka grew up to found the Zulu nation by drawing together many conquered Nguni tribal communities. During his reign as king of the amaZulu, he established a highly structured and powerful military force. He introduced new forms of traditional weapons and developed the now famous battlefield attack formation known as the 'horns of the bull'. After ten years of bloody warfare, Shaka became disliked by other Africans and by many of his own people who had suffered under his regime of war.

After the death of his mother in 1828, Shaka is thought to have become psychologically unstable, imposing a year of celibacy on his people and executing subjects who did not show due grief over her death. In the same year he was murdered by his half-brothers, Dingane (who succeeded him as ruler) and Mhlangane, and a servant, Mbhopha. In spite of claims that his reign was a brutal one, Shaka was successful in creating the large and powerful Zulu kingdom, consolidating the nation and creating a sense of national pride.

As a result of the Mfecane, there were new concentrations and groupings of people which replaced the small chiefdoms of the past. The Zulu kingdom had expanded over the lowveld of what is now KwaZulu-Natal. The Batswana and the Bapedi had migrated further north. The Swazi and the Basotho had emerged as new chiefdoms. These movements enabled Boer trekkers to move into areas which were now sparsely populated.

MOSHOESHOE I (1786 – 1870)

Moshoeshoe is widely regarded as the father of the Basotho people. The Sotho state (known today as Lesotho) began to take shape under his rule. He was distinguished for his wise, progressive and democratic leadership style, embracing dialogue rather than warfare.

In the early 1820s Moshoeshoe drew together refugees, predominantly Nguni and Sotho/Setswana speakers and Khoi-San peoples, from the Difaqane and offered them protection in the mountainous Butha-Buthe area of present-day Lesotho. After an attack in 1824 he moved his people to Thaba-Bosiu (Mountain of the Night). From here the Basotho people withstood several assaults. The mountain was never taken.

Boer soldiers from the Orange Free State did, however, capture prime farm land, and the Basotho were obliged to hand over more in a treaty in 1866. The treaty did not end the conflict, and in 1868 Moshoeshoe is said to have appealed to Queen Victoria to make his kingdom 'a flea in her blanket' as the British Protectorate of Basutoland. Some of Moshoeshoe's land was restored in the Treaty of Aliwal North in 1869. However, to this day the Basotho feel aggrieved that the land east of the Caledon River remains South African territory.

1824

Cape traders established a settlement at **Port Natal** (later Durban). At around this time also, the Cape colonial frontier was pushed as far north as the Orange River.

1829

Khoi-San families were settled in the Kat River basin, acting as a buffer against the amaXhosa on the colony's eastern frontier.

1834

Slavery was abolished to bring the colony into line with British imperial practice. The **Abolition Act of 1833** which freed all slaves in the British empire immediately did not, however, produce an instant change in the 'master-servant' relationship in the South African social economy as many slaves remained dependent on indentured labour or 'apprenticeship' for their survival. In 1838 the 'apprenticeship' system fell away and slaves were officially emancipated.

The emancipation of slaves was unpopular with Dutch-speaking settlers, many of whom chose to migrate away from British rule in what became known as the Great Trek.

THE GREAT TREK

Unhappy with British control, with the imposition of English in the colony as the language of education and administration, and the emancipation of slaves, in 1836 some 15 000 Boers began migrating in a north-easterly direction towards Natal. The movement lasted about six years. It was the first organised act of self-determination on the part of the Afrikaner people and it consolidated their growing sense of national and cultural identity. Significantly, the Boer people had come to feel that British interference (such as in the imposition of land tenure taxes and the various political reforms in the Cape) was infringing their God-given right to land and to a self-determined way of life.

Furthermore, for the Boers the abolition of slavery disrupted what they believed to be the natural order of things – that whites and blacks were not created equal and that while the former were placed on this earth to rule, the latter were here to serve. In a struggle to break the bonds of the perceived injustices, Boers headed into the interior in family and community groups, taking with them everything they owned packed into ox wagons.

In their trek into the interior, they were determined to claim ownership of land. This inevitably led to conflict in places. The majority of trekkers headed to what was later known as Natal.

The Great Trek is looked on by Afrikaners as emblematic of their flight from persecution and bid for freedom. Historians have pointed out however that about a third of their number was black and that the trekkers were assisted by Khoi-San and other African tribes, and even a number of Britons. The trekkers represented a third of the Afrikaners who actually migrated from the Cape at this time. Of these, most were poor and dispossessed.

1836

At the **Battle of Vegkop** (in the present-day northern Free State), Boer commandos defeated Mzilikazi's Ndebele forces after a series of bloody skirmishes in which the Boers were aided by the Griquas, the Barolong, the Koranna and the Batlokwa. Mzilikazi and his people were eventually forced to retreat further north across the Limpopo River. Boer commanders proceeded to seize remaining Ndebele lands and distribute Mzilikazi's considerable herd of cattle to Boer farmers. Having secured this territory the Boers set up several settlements, one of which was Potchefstroom.

1837

Dissension in trekker ranks forced a split with one group heading north and **Piet Retief** and his followers proceeding eastwards towards Port Natal.

1837

With lands seized in battles with African chiefdoms in the area, the Boers proclaimed the **Republic of Natalia** and set up an administration in the capital, Pietermaritzburg, governed by an elected volksraad (people's assembly). The state did not enjoy unanimous support among the Afrikaners and was not able to exert strong controls on the administration of the territory. It was divided on racial lines with Cape-born Dutch speakers awarding themselves rights and privileges over all others.

PIET RETIEF (1790 – 1838)
DINGANE (C.1795 – 1840) AND
ANDRIES PRETORIUS (1798 – 1853)

Piet Retief, who had led a party of trekkers from the Cape to Natal, approached Zulu King Dingane for a grant of land to settle in. Dingane, alarmed by the arrival of trekkers in such large numbers, requested Retief to recover some cattle of his which had been stolen by Sekonyela of the Batlokwa tribe, and also to capture and deliver to him Sekonyela himself.

At the meeting which followed the return of the cattle at the royal kraal at Mdungundlovu, Retief and his party were reportedly armed and agitated and **Dingane**, who was suspicious of the Boer leader, ordered the execution of the men after he had signed an agreement with them binding him to recognise the Boers' land claims. The entire party of around 100, which included around 30 black servants and many Boer women and children, were murdered.

Dingane continued to pursue an offensive policy towards white trekkers and attacked several Boer commando units. In reprisal a Boer from the Graaff-Reinet district, **Andries Pretorius**, formed a commando which comprised mainly of Boers, but also drew in some Englishmen from Port Natal, and a number of Khoi-San and local African allies. Provoking Dingane into attack, Pretorius first drew his men into a 'laager', a protective circle of wagons, on the banks of the Ncome River, from where the Boers were able to put up a formidable defence. In what became known as the **Battle of Blood River**, attacking rows of Zulu forces were systematically mown down under fire from the laager. Up to 3 000 amaZulu are believed to have been killed. No Boer casualties were recorded. The Boer victory at Blood River confirmed for the trekkers the justness of their cause. They believed this was a holy war. In a pact with God, they swore that in victory they would keep the day holy forever more.

1838

When the trekkers reached Natal, they believed they had reached the promised land. In order to settle in the region, however, they needed to reach a mutually beneficial agreement with the amaZulu who were defensive of their property and trading links.

1838

In the north, Boers proclaimed **Potchefstroom** the capital of the new Transvaal Republic.

1840

Dingane fled after his brother, **Mpande** (1798 – 1872), led a rebellion against his rule. In some disarray after their bitter defeat at Blood River, the amaZulu, like the amaXhosa before them, were unable to resist further incursions into their territory by the settlers.

Although hostilities with the white settlers persisted, Mpande consolidated and re-built the Zulu nation from the 1840s adopting a strategy of alliance and compromise with both British and Boers alike. His work continued under his successor, Cetshwayo (1826 – 1884).

1842

At first the Cape government recognised the new **Natalia** republic. Later, however, it withdrew its endorsement, uneasy about the Boer attempts to bully the local black population into submission. After the republic attempted to create a 'reserve' for surplus labourers on Pondo-held territory between the Umtamvuna and Umzimvubu Rivers in the south, the Cape government despatched a small force to protect Port Natal (later Durban) and support the amaPondo in defence of their land.

Captain Thomas Charlton Smith led the expedition in May 1842 and headed for Port Natal where he occupied what is still known today as the 'Old Fort'. Here he replaced the flag of the Natalia republic with the Union Jack. Conflict broke out leading to Smith being held siege in the Fort. **Dick King** was despatched on horseback to Grahamstown to get help for the beleaguered garrison in the Fort. His epic ride took him ten days while Smith stood firm through the siege. Ultimately Smith was relieved and in 1843 the 'Natal' district became a protectorate of the English crown and in May 1844 was annexed as a separate district of the Cape colony. Fearing British domination again, many Boers reacted by leaving the Natal region and scattering widely over the interior, frequently coming into conflict over land and livestock with settled indigenous communities.

DAVID LIVINGSTONE (1813 – 1873)

David Livingstone, an explorer, naturalist and medical missionary, arrived in South Africa in the service of the London Missionary Society in 1841. He spent the first few years of his African life based at Kuruman with Robert Moffat, whose eldest daughter, Mary, he married in 1845.

During this time and later, he undertook several exploratory adventures, seeking new missionary sites. Travelling always on foot, it has been estimated that he walked around 36 000 miles in his lifetime. He was determined to help 'open' a passage in the African continent for the spread of Christianity and Western 'civilisation'. He was known to be short-tempered with fellow European missionaries and explorers, and a passionate advocate for the abolition of slavery which persisted despite the 1833 Act of Abolition.

Livingstone became a cult figure in Britain during his lifetime. His book 'Missionary Travels' was a bestseller.

BISHOP JOHN WILLIAM COLENSO (1814 – 1893)

Consecrated in 1853, the first bishop of the new Anglican (Church of England) diocese of Natal, John Colenso conducted missionary work among the amaZulu. He translated many religious works into isiZulu and became known for his vigorous advocacy of African rights and his unorthodox theological views, in particular a tolerance of the practice of polygamy among his converts. This led to his being tried for heresy, deposed and, in 1863, excommunicated. While he was reinstated by the London court, the effect was to create a rift in the Anglican Church in South Africa and to distance the Church of England from the South African Church of England. Colenso opposed the Anglo-Zulu War and later helped to return Zulu King Cetshwayo from exile in Cape Town. In recent times, historians have reappraised Colenso's life and work and, recognising his profound contribution to the missionary project, the Anglican Church took steps to 'reinstate' him posthumously and to affirm his place in South African church history.

1847

The Cape government consolidated its occupation of Xhosa territory (kwaXhosa) by annexing **British Kaffraria** (later known as the Ciskei).

1848

The Cape government headed by Sir Harry Smith (1787 – 1860) annexed the territory between the Vaal and Orange Rivers, hoping to reach agreement with the various affected chiefdoms to protect them from Boer aggression. The proclamation of the Cape-controlled **Orange River Sovereignty** resulted in a clash between the British and the Boers, led by Andries Pretorius, at Boomplaats. Smith's forces were successful in driving Pretorius back across the Vaal River.

1852

Pretorius met with representatives of the Orange River Sovereignty at Sand River and drew up a convention providing for a British surrender of control north of the Vaal River and recognition of the area as the Boer-controlled **Zuid Afrikaansche Republiek (ZAR)**. The new republic was conceived of and developed as a whites-only domain. At the same time, the British began to withdraw from their responsibilities in the Orange River Sovereignty which was beset with problems.

1854

The **Oranje Vrystaat** (Orange Free State) was proclaimed following a meeting in Bloemfontein between local Afrikaners and a British agent. According to the terms of agreement, the British agreed to relinquish formal control over the territory. Both the OFS and the ZAR rejected the more representative British-controlled style of government in the Cape.

XHOSA CATTLE KILLINGS

An ancestral prophecy was relayed through a teenage girl named **Nongqawuse** (c.1840 - 1898) whose vision for the redemption of the nation called for sacrifices on a massive scale. Following their bitter defeat after 50-odd years of frontier wars, and in response to land losses, and to an outbreak of disease in cattle stocks, in 1856 many Xhosa chiefs ordered the mass culling of cattle and the destruction of grain harvests. This was believed to be an act of ritual purification and sanctioned by the ancestors.

Most of the Xhosa cattle stocks were destroyed as the injunction was carried out. When no obvious act of national regeneration followed the cattle killings, and with tens of thousands of amaXhosa facing starvation, many were forced to migrate west to the colony in search of work as labourers. Of those that stayed, it is thought that some 40 000 died of starvation.

With the decimation of the amaXhosa, white occupation and agricultural development progressed rapidly on formerly Xhosa-held lands. Today this area is known as the eastern Cape.

1856

The **Charter of Natal** separated Natal from the administrative authority of the Cape, and gave the province some independence and political authority over its own affairs. The charter made provision for open franchise. However, despite influxes of English settlers, Natal whites were less tolerant of the multi-racial ideals of the Cape, and racist attitudes soon entrenched themselves.

1860s

Indentured labourers, mostly lower caste Indian men and women from Madras, arrived in Natal on low-paying five-year indentured contracts to labour in the newly-planted sugar plantations in Natal. After the expiry of their contracts, many chose to stay on and make a new life for themselves.

Natal's Secretary for Native Affairs, **Theophilus Shepstone** (1817 - 1893) implemented a segregationist administration in Natal, creating 'reserves' for Africans and arguing that the system would protect and promote African indigenous culture. Spread widely throughout the territory, the 'reserves' made it possible for the white minority to control more effectively the black majority, and provided convenient sources of cheap labour to white farmers.

1867

Two boys discovered **diamonds** in the Hopetown area near the Orange River. This led to a rapid influx of prospectors to the area and development of many small towns in the diamond fields around Kimberley. From 1871 hundreds of thousands of Africans streamed into the area and were enlisted into the diamond cash economy.

CECIL JOHN RHODES (1853 – 1902)

Cecil John Rhodes was both loved and hated for his imperial dream of annexing further African territory for Britain, and for his meteoric rise to power and influence in the region following a humble start in the Kimberley diamond diggings. In 1875, at a time of market saturation and with a plummeting of the diamond price, Rhodes bought up many claimants' pitches after they collapsed. This gave him and his company, **De Beers Consolidated**, a substantial stake in the Kimberley mines in the inevitable market upturn. With his considerable wealth he was able to buy himself political position at the Cape, becoming premier of the colony in 1890.

He sought to monopolise the gold of the Rand and masterminded the so-called 'Jameson Raid' aiming to overthrow the Transvaal government. With the failure of the raid in 1895, Rhodes contributed to a growing mistrust between Afrikaans and English speakers, and was in part responsible for the terrible war fought between Britain and the Afrikaners from 1899 to 1902.

After his death Rhodes was revered by some for his personal magnetism and his grandiose dreams, and for his work in building institutions and developing communications in the region. By many others, however, he was held in scorn for ruthlessly pursuing entrepreneurial and imperial advancement at the expense of the basic human rights of Africans in the region.

With the discovery of diamonds, the British reversed their informal policies of co-operative detachment from the Boer states and adopted a more interventionist approach.

1870s

At this time South Africa consisted of the two British colonies of the Cape and Natal, and the two Boer republics of the Orange Free State and the South African Republic (ZAR/Transvaal). British Colonial Secretary, **Lord Carnarvon** (1830 – 1890), conceived the idea of a confederation of these colonies and states in order to bring some semblance of order, a common Native policy and increased British influence to the southern African territory.

1877

In pursuit of this policy of **confederation**, the British dispatched Sir Theophilus Shepstone to annex the South African Republic as the British colony of the Transvaal. The move, which was supposed to be temporary, had the support of the economically powerful British residents of the Transvaal, as well as a significant number of Boers who hoped that this would offer them some protection against Bapedi and Venda attempts to re-impose their control over northern and eastern parts of the republic. Dissatisfaction with British rule in the republic grew steadily however.

1877

Skirmishes over land rights between the amaZulu, and British and Boer settlers in northern Natal persisted under Zulu **King Cetshwayo** (1826 – 1884).

THE ZULU WAR

In a move to disarm and control the amaZulu, British colonial forces invaded **Zululand, now KwaZulu-Natal.** This lead to a battle at **Isandlwana** in 1879 in which British forces were convincingly routed by Zulu impis (soldiers), despite suffering massive casualties. In a dramatic coincidence, while the battle was underway the scene was shrouded in darkness by a total solar eclipse.

The victory at Isandlwana has acquired symbolic significance for Zulu-speaking people of South Africa and for black South Africans generally, and is still upheld today as a mighty blow against the invasive colonial forces at work in the region.

Zulu and British soldiers clashed again at **Rorke's Drift** later the same day, where the British successfully repulsed a concerted attack on a small hospital and supply depot.

The war lasted six months, with more Zulu successes at the battles of Hlobane and Intombi Spruit. They also laid siege to a British garrison at Eshowe for two months. British victories at Nyezane, Khambule and Gingindlovu caused severe Zulu casualties, and the final battle of the war, the Battle of Ulundi, effectively ended organised Zulu military resistance. After this battle, the British burned the nearby kwaZulu capital, Ondini, to the ground. Cetshwayo eluded the British for several months, but was eventually captured and exiled to the Cape.

1879

Soon after the defeat of the Zulus, the British defeated the **Bapedi** in the north. The Bapedi had put up a valiant fight against Boer, Zulu, Swazi and British attempts to destroy their autonomy. Their conquest, however, gave the British control over the lands of the north and access to the potential labour forces who lived on it.

1880

The British then turned their attention to subjugating the **Basotho**. They were met with ferocious local resistance but were eventually successful in securing their land.

1880

Boer resistance to the annexation of the South African Republic (Transvaal) in 1877 led to the **First Anglo-Boer War** (also known as the Transvaal War of Independence). In a skirmish at Majuba Mountain, a British unit was roundly defeated by a small Boer commando, leading ultimately to Britain relinquishing control over the South African Republic. What followed was a significant kindling of Afrikaner nationalist spirit which took much of its definition from its opposition to British culture and influence, and its increasingly anti-African sentiments.

1880

The **Afrikaner Bond** was formed in the Cape colony. This followed a revival in Afrikaner nationalism which held that the Afrikaners were a chosen people, destined by God to rule over southern Africa and its native inhabitants. The organisation aimed to mobilise Afrikaners in the Cape, Transvaal and OFS into a broad-based body united by common political, cultural, religious and linguistic aspirations. While the Bond advocated ethnic self-determinism and sought to bring an end to British dominion in the Transvaal, it was to an extent committed to working alongside the British and in the 1890s was successful in enlisting the support of some English speakers in the Cape. Under the leadership of **Jan Hofmeyr (1845 – 1909)**, it was also successful in gaining a minority footing in the Cape parliament.

1883

In order to forestall any resurgence of Zulu military might, the Zulu nation was fragmented into 13 sub-chiefdoms under a British administration. This led to severe inter-group rivalries and eventually to civil war. In 1883 at a meeting on the Isle of Wight, **Cetshwayo** successfully petitioned Queen Victoria for his return to Zululand. The British administration welcomed his return in the vain hope that he would diffuse the conflict. Tensions continued unabated however. The king died in 1883 leaving his son **Dinuzulu** on the throne. With ongoing conflict in his kingdom, Dinuzulu enlisted Boer military support against his main antagonist, Zibephu. The consequence of the alliance with the Boers was the allocation of a large portion of Zululand to the Boers who established farms in the territory.

1883

Paul Kruger (1825 – 1904) became president of the Transvaal republic (ZAR).

1884

The British annexed the territory known as the **Transkei** to the Cape in its campaign to protect their interests elsewhere in the region.

1885

The British annexed **Bechuanaland** (now Botswana) in an effort to pre-empt German colonial expansion from its foothold in south-western Africa (now Namibia).

1886

Gold was discovered on the Witwatersrand, 30 miles south of Pretoria, leading to a massive influx of speculators, investors and prospectors to the site, now known as **Johannesburg**. The supply seemed inexhaustible but as operators mined to greater depths, the costs of extracting gold ore rose sharply. Larger and more powerful mining companies swallowed up most of the smaller operators and the Transvaal government imposed strict controls on the industry.

1887

Continued friction in **Zululand** eventually led the British to annex the territory in 1887, and it was administered as such until 1897 when it became part of the colony of Natal. In terms of the annexation proclamation, Zululand was declared to consist of 'unalienated Crown land' to which the amaZulu were to have unhindered access. It also contained a clause prohibiting white settlement for a period of five years. In 1903 and 1904 Zululand was carved up into separate areas for black and white settlers by the Zululand Lands Delimitation Commission.

DIAMONDS AND GOLD

The discovery of diamonds and gold totally altered the history of the region. It led to rapid urbanisation and investment, and to the development of infrastructure and industry resulting in a shift in economic dominance away from the Cape and towards the Boer states. Ultimately it led to the development of a more cohesive state drawing together the disparate colonies in what later became the four provinces of the Union and Republic of South Africa.

Under the republican premiership of Paul Kruger, thousands of Africans were conscripted to labour on the mines, their employment contracts and wages subject to the vagaries of the new market, of labour supply and demand and government controls.

The new town of Johannesburg grew rapidly and from the earliest days was characterised by a growing division between the haves and the have-nots. It was dominated by mine-owning, middle-class English speakers, known as the Uitlanders, who were denied the right to vote or stand for office in the Transvaal republic.

PAUL KRUGER (1825 – 1904)

Born in 1825 in Colesberg in the Cape colony, **Paul Kruger**, who never received a day's formal schooling in his life, came to be known by his people as a fearless hunter and adventurer and, as a military commander, to be the bravest man in the Boer commandos. As a statesman and president of the South African Republic (ZAR) he was famous in both Europe and Africa for his strenuous defence of the independence of the Boer republic.

All his life, Kruger had opposed the British. At the time of the gold rush, Afrikaner resentment against the British grew sharply, pivoting on the exclusion of the Uitlanders from the political process in the republic. With the British annexation of the ZAR in 1877, he led a successful campaign resulting in his succession to the office of State President in 1883.

Kruger's government of the republic was based on strictly biblical foundations. He was single-minded in his determination to stave off outside interference in the affairs of the republic. In this stance, he was vehemently supported by his loyal constituents, most of whom lived off the land and were granted favours by his regime. For many he became a folk hero and a spiritual leader.

Kruger is partly remembered as a conservationist in his efforts to create a sanctuary for wildlife in the Transvaal in 1898 (the **Kruger National Park**). Having in his earlier years been a voracious big game hunter (killing by his own estimate between 30 and 40 elephants, five lions and numerous other big game animals), he is said to have come to the realisation that most species of big game would cease to exist in South Africa if they were not protected in a safe haven.

In the South African War (1899 – 1902), Kruger, who was by then in his 70s, exerted strong central leadership for the Boer commandos. In the three-year war, the Boers secured several early victories. Increasingly, however, they came under duress, as the British forces adopted more offensive strategies. In May 1899 Kruger was forced to abandon Pretoria in the face of an advancing enemy. For a while he led a mobile government. Eventually he was shipped off to Europe – a decision that was made to prevent the leader from falling into enemy hands.

He died as a refugee in 1904 in Switzerland, two years after the South African Republic lost its independence.

THE JAMESON RAID

With mounting Uitlander grievances at being excluded from the political process and being subject to stringent controls and taxes, Cape premier Cecil Rhodes together with several other leading mine representatives hatched a plot in 1895 to engineer a rebellion aimed at overthrowing the Kruger administration.

The plan was that **Leander Starr Jameson** (1853 – 1917), together with a small armed force, would enter the area from Bechuanaland and use the rebellion to effect a coup in the Transvaal state.

The plan failed when the rebellion failed to materialise and Jameson and his men were apprehended soon after setting foot on Transvaal territory. The failed raid further undermined British Afrikaner relations and set the tone for a climate which evolved steadily towards war.

1896 – 1897

A **rinderpest** epidemic – which had followed the movement of cattle from east Africa right across the west coast and down into southern Africa – wiped out up to 90% of livestock in the region. This further impoverished local African communities who were already under pressure to capitulate to imperial forces through colonial state taxes and pressures to enter the migrant labour system.

1897

Lord Alfred Milner (1854 - 1925) became Cape Governor and British High Commissioner to South Africa and immediately embarked on a smear campaign against Paul Kruger, making every effort to undermine the Transvaal government ostensibly in his promotion of 'fair treatment for British industry and capital in the Transvaal'. To this end the Cape government put out the notion that the Uitlanders were an oppressed minority in the Transvaal.

1899

In May a meeting in Bloemfontein was convened by OFS premier, M T Steyn (1857 – 1916), with the aim of bringing together Kruger and Milner to resolve their differences. The two leaders failed to reach any sort of compromise or understanding. **Tensions escalated** rapidly and both the Transvaal and the British governments began positioning themselves for the war that followed.

Following the amassing of British troops along the Cape-Natal borders in October, Kruger presented the British with an **ultimatum** demanding their withdrawal within 48 hours. The ultimatum was ignored and the Transvaal government declared war on Britain.

1899 – 1902

The South African War

Both sides of the South African War (also known as the Boer War, the Anglo-Boer War and to some, the Second War of Independence) believed they were defending their national integrity. For the British, which had failed to absorb the two Boer republics into a British controlled confederation in the late 1870s, the 'discovery' of gold threatened to allow the South African Republic political and economic dominance in the country. Hitherto Britain had been the most influential power in the area through its control of its two colonies of the Cape and Natal, and the Protectorates of Basutoland and Bechuanaland.

OLIVE SCHREINER (1855 – 1920)

Born to missionary parents in Basutoland (now Lesotho), Olive Schreiner became a sharp critic of British imperialism and racism in South Africa. She had been a friend of Cecil Rhodes but turned away from him when she found herself unable to share his political and social convictions, and unable to support the armed rising that led to the war in 1899.

Olive Schreiner found herself ostracised by the establishment for her anti-war sentiments. Her house was burned down with her manuscripts in it, and she was interned for a year because of her public support for the Afrikaner cause. After the war, she formed the Women's Enfranchisement League in Cape Town in 1908 and in 1911 reconstructed the lost manuscript into a book, 'Women and Labour' that would make her internationally famous.

Schreiner rose to international fame as a major South African writer of fiction, as an eloquent advocate of feminism, socialism, pacifism and free thought, and as a trenchant critic of British imperialism and racism. Although she wrote political and social treatises, allegories and short stories, she is perhaps best known for her novel 'The Story of an African Farm'.

The Boer fighters were vigorously supported by Boer women in the war. Bitterly angered by the looting and burning of their homes, Boer women put up a formidable defence of their homes, families and national pride. They urged their men into action on the war fronts while courageously, if not vainly, fending off British attacks on their homes.

African families and communities were also frequently caught up in the destruction of the war, and experienced displacement and dispossession as the war progressed.

Both sides conscripted local black men into service as either combatants or field auxiliaries. It is estimated that black people made up over 20% of the republican fighting force – giving the lie to the notion that this was 'a white man's war'. After the war their contribution was largely forgotten.

In the distraction of war, some Zulu, Pedi, Venda and Tswana communities used the opportunity to seize back territory previously lost in skirmishes with colonial and settler forces. Some were successful but many gains were reversed after the war.

First phase of the war (1899 – 1900)

Under the command of **Piet Joubert** in the Transvaal and **Piet Cronje** in the OFS, the republican forces claimed many early victories in the war. The Boer commandos proved to be a formidable enemy for the British, well armed with Mauser rifles and heavy field artillery.

In the early phases of the war, the republican forces laid siege to the towns of **Kimberley**, **Ladysmith** and **Mafeking**, holding hostage hundreds of British military and civilian personnel. Efforts to relieve these towns led to bloody clashes and decisive victories for the Boers, particularly at Stormberg, Magersfontein, near Kimberley, and at Colenso and Spioenkop in Natal.

SOL PLAATJE (1876 – 1932)

One of those caught up in the siege of Mafeking was Sol Plaatje, a prolific diarist, journalist and author who later became the first general secretary of the South African Native National Congress (which later became the African National Congress/ANC) when it was founded in 1912. At the time of the siege, Plaatje was employed as a court interpreter at Mafeking. His diarised account of the siege was first published in 1984.

As a journalist Plaatje saw his role as providing a mouthpiece for African aspirations of the era. In 1916 he published a political tract angrily denouncing the 1913 Natives' Land Act (Native Life in South Africa). He began by saying "Awakening on Friday morning, June 20 1913, the South African native found himself...a pariah in the land of his birth." Plaatje wrote prolifically in both English and Setswana and is widely remembered today as the author of the first novel in English to be written by a black South African (Mhudi). As one of the early ANC leaders, he distinguished himself as a political spokesperson and an official diplomat for the ANC cause.

In order to effect a reversal in their fortunes, Britain deployed **General Horatio Kitchener** (1850 – 1916) to the field as second-in-command to **Field Marshall 'Bobs' Roberts** (1832 – 1914). The move was somewhat successful for the British in that it led to the relief of the three towns, and to offensive operations which put considerable pressure on the Boer commandos, forcing some into retreat.

After the Orange Free State was occupied and annexed to Britain, British forces made for the Transvaal where they captured both Johannesburg and Pretoria. Within three months, Britain annexed the Transvaal and General Kruger had been displaced from his seat of power in Pretoria. Lord Roberts, declaring a victory, had returned home in 1900 leaving Kitchener to oversee what became the deadliest phase of the war.

Second phase of the war (1900 – 1902)

The second phase of the South African War saw Boer commandos fighting in smaller units and with recourse to the tactics of guerrilla warfare. Commandos moved quickly through the territory, attacking strategic targets and receiving support and shelter from a large network of Boer farms.

As a counter strategy, **Kitchener** devised a plan to fence off large blocks of territory with the aim of isolating the enemy commandos. Furthermore he continued and extended Roberts' scorched earth policy, indiscriminately setting fire to Boer farms and settlements. Victims, mostly women and children, were rounded up and sheltered in **concentration camps**. Separate camps were created for displaced African families. By 1901, tens of thousands were held in the camps in conditions which did nothing to alleviate the suffering of the victims. More than 20 000 people died of disease and starvation in the camps, one in five of these a child.

EMILY HOBHOUSE (1860 – 1926)

News reaching Britain of the concentration camps prompted a British Quaker and anti-war campaigner, Emily Hobhouse, to establish the non-sectarian 'South African Women and Children's Distress Fund', and to travel to South Africa in 1900 to oversee its distribution. Milner permitted her to travel to the camps but Kitchener refused to allow her to travel further than Bloemfontein. She was able to visit several camps, though none in the Transvaal, and made personal contact with women held in them. She provided extensive eye-witness accounts of the suffering of the people in the camps. Finding that there was a scarcity of the most basic provisions (like soap), she had some success in securing improvements in the conditions and in raising British public awareness about barbarous methods being employed in the 'South African campaign'.

Emily Hobhouse became an honorary South African through her coura-geous exposure of conditions in the camps. In 1913, she was invited – but was too ill to travel – to Bloemfontein for the unveiling of a monument to the victims of the concentration camps. At the ceremony her speech was read in her absence. In it, she issued a prophetic call to all South Africans:

"Be merciful towards the weak, the down-trodden, the stranger. Do not open your gates to those worst foes of freedom – tyranny and selfishness. Are not these the withholding from others in your control, the very liberties and rights which you have valued and won for yourselves?"

Emily Hobhouse's ashes are interred at the foot of the Women's Memorial monument in Bloemfontein.

The guerrilla commandos were unable to hold out indefinitely against Kitchener's strategy. While many went on to resist British efforts to subjugate them to the 'bitter end', by the end of 1901 Boer leaders agreed to enter peace talks with the British. On 31 May 1902, the Boers surrendered to the British and peace was secured in the **Vereeniging Treaty**.

The tragedy of war

The South African War caused untold destruction, loss and human suffering. Tens of thousands of people died, many from disease. Homesteads and communities were destroyed. Families were broken up and displaced. The war has come to be viewed as a needless and wasteful loss of life and property.

In the peace settlement, the way was cleared and resources were provided for Milner to embark on an extensive programme of reconstruction and development, albeit one which ignored African aspirations. While the British had succeeded in attaining economic and political control, and in bringing all four colonies under common administration, they had not been successful in subjugating the Afrikaner sense of nationhood and cultural pride.

Under the peace treaty, Boer prisoners of war were repatriated, Afrikaans was restored to use in schools, and the courts and Boer property and land claims were recognised. African compensation claims were barely recognised, however. The British gave assurances that self-rule for the Afrikaners would remain high on the agenda and that the franchise would not be extended to the African majority before self-rule had been successfully negotiated. In the years following the war, Afrikaner nationalist aspirations therefore began once again to flourish.

Together, however, the Afrikaners and the British were able to co-operate in laying the foundations for a powerful modern economy founded on a principle of racial segregation and exploitation, and on the denial of political and economic rights to the African majority.

CHAPTER 6

THE 20TH CENTURY

The Union

1900 – 1948

The reconstruction and development campaign overseen by Lord Alfred Milner at the beginning of the 20th century amounted to an industrial and agricultural revolution in South Africa. But while white farmers were enabled to undertake agricultural production on a commercial scale, black farmers who did not benefit from start-up support on the same scale were barely able to rise from subsistence production. Instead many black subsistence farmers found themselves excluded from the mainstream commercial economy and instead pressured into the labour economy. Furthermore in an affirmative action programme, jobless and poor whites were provided with sheltered employment in specially conceived job creation projects.

For most of the 20th century ahead the African majority was to face ongoing disempowerment and a constant battle simply to survive. In the 1800s most food was grown by black, formerly subsistence farmers, mainly sharecroppers, including that food sold on the market. It was only with the Land Act, hut taxes and indirect rule and subsidies from government for whites that forced peasant labourers to become migrant labourers for white farmers.

1903

Milner instructed the **South African Native Affairs Commission** to draw up a 'native policy'. The resulting report totally ignored the opinions and aspirations of the African, coloured and Indian representatives to the Commission. The report advocated, among many other things, a consolidation of Shepstone's policy of a separate 'native' administration and the introduction of a **pass system** to control the movement of Africans. The report influenced several successive administrations in the country and laid the basis for the total repression of the 'non-white' majority in the country in the decades to come.

1904

Over 60 000 **indentured Chinese labourers** were imported to the Rand to work on the gold mines on three-year contracts, significantly undercutting African labour demands. Gold production soared. While the experiment was successful, most of the Chinese labourers were repatriated in 1907 following a public outcry in London over reports of conditions in the labour compounds.

1906

Along with a denial of black civil rights, and growing and blatant levels of race discrimination in the country, the Natal government levied a £1 **poll tax** on all unmarried males, black and white. This tax was implemented with the aim of forcing men to take part in the labour market. Some communities ignored the tax. Others responded with defiance.

THE BAMBATHA UPRISING

In a rebellion against the poll tax, the deaths of two white policemen in Zululand precipitated a brutal response from the state who tracked down and summarily executed suspects. In turn, this provoked a full-scale uprising organised by a Zulu chief, Bambatha (d.1906) in which thousands of Africans, mainly amaZulu, took up arms against the white British authorities. The rebellion, which took place in waves, was systematically crushed by the authorities. More than 3 000 Africans, all male, and around 30 whites were killed in the uprising. In the final battle which took place in the Nkandla forest in 'Zululand', Bambatha himself was reported to have been killed. When a white sergeant was sent to the forest to obtain positive identification, the corpse was decapitated and the head carried back to Nkandla for identification. Although the head was reliably identified, there remained a strong belief among the amaZulu that Bambatha had in fact escaped to Mozambique where he lived and eventually died.

The Bambatha uprising was the last attempt at armed resistance for many years to come. It had stunned and frightened white Natal and prepared the ground for an Afrikaans and English political alliance to meet further black resistance.

1906

Autonomy was returned to the Orange Free State and the Transvaal. In local elections in 1907, Afrikaner majorities were returned in both states. In the Transvaal, the succeeding Het Volk (The People) party, led by **Generals Louis Botha (1862 – 1919)** and **Jan Smuts (1870 – 1950)**, instigated a deliberate policy of conciliation with English speakers.

1907

Sir Percy Fitzpatrick, an Irishman seeking his fortune in South Africa accompanied by his faithful companion, Jock, a Bull Terrier, published his famous tale of their adventures in *Jock of the Bushveld*.

1908

A **National Convention** comprising 14 Afrikaner and 16 British delegates (and no others) met in Durban and Cape Town to negotiate a constitution for a new South African state. The terms of the constitution entrenched white supremacy under a unitary state. No effort was made to extend the Cape franchise to Africans. Protests made by an official African delegation to London – led by writer John Jabavu (1859 – 1921) – were effectively ignored.

1909

Among the protests at the proposed new constitution was that of the newly-formed elite **African Political Organisation (APO)**. Cape-based, the group principally represented the interests of 'Coloured' South Africans which it believed to be distinct from African political interests.

1909

The British parliament ratified the new constitution and passed the **South Africa Act** without any dissension. The Act transferred power in perpetuity to minority white voters, and the country was granted judicial independence.

THE UNION OF SOUTH AFRICA

In 1910 the colonies (Cape, Natal, Transvaal, OFS) merged to form a Union. South Africa – as a political state with a national political identity – came into being.

In an attempt to off-set the centralisation of power, the new state would be administered from three different centres, namely the parliament in Cape Town, the judiciary based in Bloemfontein, and the executive based in Pretoria.

To begin with, the British government insisted that the new state would exclude the protectorates of Bechuanaland, Basutholand and Swaziland. These would be incorporated only when and if the 'native policy' met with British approval. However when the South African state broke ties with the Commonwealth in the 1960s, each was proclaimed independent as Botswana and the Kingdoms of Lesotho and Swaziland.

At the first whites-only national elections, **General Louis Botha** (1862 – 1919) was put into power as Prime Minister. Under his administration, a policy of racial segregation in every sphere of private and civic life began to take shape, and over the next few decades was systematically enacted by parliament.

1911

The **Mines and Works Act of 1911** which imposed the industrial colour bar on the Rand made it impossible for black workers to obtain skilled work, which was reserved for whites. This was not only true of the mines, but other trades also.

1912

The Afrikaaner Nationalist Party, the forerunner to the National Party, was formed by **General J B M Hertzog** (1866 – 1942) and dedicated itself to making South Africa a racially-segregated republic. In the very same year, the ANC was born, in the founding of the South African Native National Congress (SANNC), and dedicated itself to uniting Africans in the fight against injustice and equal rights.

THE SOUTH AFRICAN NATIVE NATIONAL CONGRESS

On 8 January 1912, the **Reverend John Langalibalele Dube** (1871 – 1946), a headmaster and editor of the newspaper *Ilanga Lase Natal*, founded the South African Native National Congress in Bloemfontein in response to the Union government's blatant disregard of civil rights for Africans (which by now had extended to Indians in Natal). With Sol Plaatje as the first General Secretary, the Congress was liberal in outlook and committed to defending what few African civil rights remained. It attracted middle-class, missionary-educated African men, many of them traditional leaders, as well as teachers, ministers and journalists.

At this stage it was not a mass movement. Indeed it distanced itself from popular protests against discriminatory legislation. The modus operandi was conciliatory rather than confrontational, petitioning rather than protesting. One of the SANNC petitions was for the extension of the Cape franchise throughout the union. The moderate tactics espoused by the Congress rendered it unable to effectively influence either local or British 'native' policy. However, it held enormous symbolic significance. While smaller national African congresses were already in existence (e.g. the 1900 formation of the Natal Native Congress), its formation was the first truly national attempt to unite the expression of African aspirations under one umbrella. In 1923 the Congress changed its name to the **African National Congress (ANC)**.

1913

Mahatma Gandhi (1869 – 1948) led a great protest march against a plethora of grievances held by Asian South Africans. The protest was sparked by the Botha government's attempt to bar further immigration from south Asia and to declare future immigrants as 'undesirables'.

MAHATMA GANDHI (1869 – 1948)

Born in Gujarat, M K Gandhi practised at the London bar in the 1890s before arriving in South Africa in 1893 to represent the legal interests of an Indian merchant company. He remained in South Africa for another 21 years.

Like most other Indian-born South Africans, Gandhi was the victim of stinging and humiliating racist attacks, most famously when he was thrown out of a first-class (whites-only) carriage at the Pietermaritzburg train station. His experiences in South Africa led him to abandon his loyalty to the British empire and his attachment to Western perspectives and ways of being, and embrace instead an asceticism founded on his evolving philosophy of *satyagraha* ('soul-force'). Gandhi is reputed to have once said, when asked what he thought of Western Civilisation, that he thought it would be 'a good idea'.

Satyagraha was a form of passive resistance which Gandhi enacted in his life and leadership both in South Africa and later in India. It involved quietly refusing to obey unjust laws and accepting the consequences for doing so.

The 1913 protest united a variety of other grievances held by impoverished Indian labourers in Natal at the time including the restrictions on owning property and on the right to enter the Cape, Orange Free State and Transvaal. Protests took the form of a deliberate flouting of the law, non-payment of taxes and burning of passes. The unarmed protesters, including Gandhi himself, were rounded up and imprisoned. While some concessions were eventually forthcoming, others were not. Restrictions on trading, property ownership and the freedom of movement remained in place.

1913

The **Natives' Land Act of 1913** was passed. It laid the basis for a spacial separation of whites and Africans, demarcating land as either 'white' or 'native' and destroying a thriving African land-owning and peasant agricultural sector. Seven percent of land was allocated to traditional reserves. The Act effectively gave 13% of the land to 87% of the people. At the same time, it gave whites unhindered access to the remaining land and made available a number of incentive schemes for white farmers to develop their land agriculturally.

Up until this time white farmers were able to lease land to black tenants, who then paid them half of their crops as rental in a **sharecropping** system. This was now illegal although in some areas of the country it continued on the quiet.

During this time the system of **migrant labour** became more common. Rural Africans would leave their families to work on white farms, on the mines or in towns because their plots were insufficient to provide food for their families and were frequently beset with problems related to drought and overgrazing, or they were forced to enter the labour market through initiatives like hut taxes. Seen as 'single' men, they were paid very little and the exploitation of their labour subsidised the development of white agriculture and industry.

On the Rand **mine protests** developed among white miners against their replacement by cheap migrant labour. Black miners protested against pass controls and unequal treatment, despite these protests being ruthlessly crushed. While white miners had the right to strike, blacks did not. Brutal physical attacks on black migrants were commonplace on the mines and in the towns.

1913

Strikes and protests against the **pass laws** were widespread at this time. Women in the Orange Free State took the lead in a mass protest in July 1913 when they marched to the municipal offices in Bloemfontein and deposited a bag containing their passes. In Winburg, President of the SANNC Women's League, **Charlotte Manye Maxeke** (1874 – 1939), was arrested along with 800 other women on an anti-pass march to the town hall.

1914

The **National Party (NP)** was formed by **General Hertzog** who had been a leading light in the Afrikaner lobby against the Union's involvement in the Great War. Hertzog said about Smuts (see 1919 on p. 55) that his 'footsteps dripped with the blood of his own people'. The National Party was established specifically to develop Afrikaner national interests. Among these was a separation from the British Empire.

THE GREAT WAR (1914 – 1918)

The First World War was waged in Europe between Britain and Germany and their respective allies. As a dominion state of the empire, South Africans were called on to fight for the British cause. While the government, under the South African Party headed by Prime Minister Louis Botha, supported this cause, there were many groups in the country that opposed the war. Some believed in African neutrality; others, hard-line Afrikaners who perceived Germany to be their natural ally, felt that South Africa was entering the war on the wrong side. This lobby led to a rebellion in the western Transvaal.

Black and coloured South Africans were conscripted in small numbers. While some saw active combat on the African and European war fronts, most were deployed as auxiliary workers and servants.

Soon after the war started, **German South West Africa** (today Namibia) was occupied following a clash between British and German colonial forces along the German colony's border with South Africa. In 1920 the Union government was mandated to administer the territory, a mandate which was renewed under a United Nations trusteeship agreement after the Second World War. The South African administration continued until the independence of Namibia some 75 years later.

1917

The **Industrial Workers of Africa (IWA)** was founded by the International Socialist League in Johannesburg. This was the first industrial African trade union.

1918

The **Industrial and Commercial Union (ICU)** was formed in Cape Town by dock workers. Under the leadership of **Clements Kadalie** (1896 – 1951), it began to organise local labour movements and actions under one umbrella. It enjoyed enormous popular support and success in raising campaigns on a number of political, social and labour issues, becoming a thorn in the flesh for the state and the establishment. The formation of the ICU was the first expression of a broad-based national labour movement in South Africa.

1918

The government temporarily suspended efforts to enforce pass laws on women.

1919

General Jan Smuts (1870 – 1950) took over as Prime Minister after the death of Louis Botha. Smuts, a great philosopher and a man of somewhat liberal sentiments, was recognised for his international statesmanship, having participated in the drawing up of the Treaty at Versailles at the end of the war. He was seen by many people at home, however, to indulge his 'diplomatic' career at the expense of dealing with domestic problems, in which he developed a reputation for ruthlessness.

1919

Around 70 000 **African miners** went on strike on the Rand. Troops and armed whites broke up meetings and barricades. In total 11 strikers were killed and over 120 wounded.

1921

The state was steadily gaining a reputation for its ruthless and brutal suppression of opposition. In the **Bulhoek massacre**, 183 people were shot dead on 4 May 1921 when state forces opened fire on a religious group known as the 'Israelites' who had gathered at Bulhoek (near Queenstown) to await a millenarian event which prophesied the expulsion of whites from the land. The massacre is said to have taken 10 minutes.

As rural communities pressed up harder against drought, harvest failures and famine, more and more people gravitated to millenarian movements which promised the return of Zion and salvation from white oppression. This heralded the rapid rise of the **African Independent Church movement** in South Africa.

1921

The **Communist Party of South Africa (CPSA)** was formed. The CPSA began a loose alliance with the ANC, working together on various campaigns of defiance against the enactment of discriminatory laws.

THE RAND REVOLT

In 1922, white mine workers embarked on a general strike on the Reef in defence of their jobs, after mine owners reduced wage costs and announced their intention to drop the industrial colour bar. For two months the mines were shut down. When the strikers marched on Johannesburg, capturing the city hall, General Smuts declared a state of martial law and the army and air force were used to disperse crowds and break up the strike. Pitched battles raged in Johannesburg for a week before Smuts stepped in again and the revolt was crushed.

In what became known as 'The Rand Revolt', more than 214 strikers and enforcement officers were killed after a work stoppage by 20 000 white mine and power station workers. During this time as many as 30 Africans were killed by white vigilantes. As a result of the strike, proposals to place blacks into jobs reserved for whites were dropped by mine owners, thus perpetuating the supremacy of white workers in the mining industry.

One of the outcomes of the revolt was that the Smuts government began to lose support from its own constituency.

1923

The **Native (Black) Urban Areas Act** was passed entrenching the pass system and officially segregating Africans in separate urban areas known as 'locations'. It became impossible for black people to own land in towns and cities. Furthermore their presence in white areas was controlled by 'the wants of the white population'.

1923

As many as 52 people were killed when state troops opened fire in South-West-Africa on a protest by the **Bondelswarts** (a group of Khoi-Khoi/Basters) against the imposition of a heavy new dog tax.

1924

A coalition between the National Party (under Hertzog) and the Labour Party (under Frederick Creswell (1866 – 1948) came into power. The **Pact government** set about furthering the segregationist policies of the earlier

Botha regime. A new national flag replaced the Union Jack and moves were
made to improve the lot of Afrikaners through job creation schemes. Afrikaans
speakers were put into the civil service wherever possible.

1925

Under Hertzog's government, Afrikaans replaced Dutch as a joint official
language. Furthermore a whole plethora of **Native Bills** were put in place
allowing for greater control of the white authorities over the black majority.
Among these was the **Native Administration Act of 1927** which imposed a
government-appointed rule by chiefs in 'tribal reserves'.

1926

Extension of the colour bar to private business was made possible through the
Mines and Workers Amendment Act of 1926.

The **Industrial Conciliation Act of 1924** allowed whites, coloureds and Indians
to form legally registered trade unions, but barred Africans from organising in
this way.

1927

Sex between whites and Africans was made illegal by the Hertzog
government. Coloureds and Indians were later included in this prohibition
during 1949 and 1950, when the Prohibition of Mixed Marriages and the
Immorality Acts were passed.

1929

South African exports were strongly affected by the **Great Depression**
(1929 – 1933) which followed the Wall Street crash. Industry and agriculture
were affected as the gold price slumped and market demands fell as prices
rose. The economy, with gold as its mainspring, recovered with the 1933
devaluation of the dollar and sterling. As a result of state intervention, in the
form of various developments (such as, for example, the creation of Iscor and
Eskom), white-controlled industry boomed while the rural black economy
languished, pushing more and more people into acute poverty.

1929

The Federation of Afrikaans Cultural Organisations (**Federasie van Afrikaans Kultuurverenigings/FAK**) was formed to further the development of Afrikaans as a language and Afrikaner cultural life. This was an initiative of the Afrikaner Broederbond, a cultural and political movement started in South Africa just after the First World War.

1930

White women were given the vote.

1931

South Africa was given more independent standing by a **Statute of Westminster** which conferred its autonomy within the British empire.

1932

South Africa left the gold standard.

1934

Another fusion government was formed, this time between Hertzog's National Party and Smuts' South African Party. Together they formed the **United Party** headed by Hertzog as Prime Minister. This marked a departure from the Afrikaner separatism of the previous regime and prompted **Dr Daniel François Malan** (1874 – 1959), who was outraged at the English-Afrikaans government alliance, to form the 'Purified' National Party (the **Herenigde Nasionale Party (HNP)**. The HNP made a vigorous stand for independence from Britain and for the mobilisation of all Afrikaners into one political, cultural and social entity. In this Malan was backed by the Afrikaner Broederbond. The new party steadily gained support, and changed its name to the 'National Party' during the Second World War.

THE AFRIKANER BROEDERBOND

Started initially after the First World War in 1919, as an Afrikaner cultural movement, the Broederbond grew steadily in its membership, attracting exclusively white Afrikaner males from the clergy, business, professional and political life. The Broederbond, which acted something like a secret society, steadily gained influence in the politics and administration and in a wide range of civic institutions in the country. It attracted Afrikaners who shared Malan's belief that the Afrikaner people were a chosen race and destined to a place of total domination in South Africa. From this time until the presidency of Nelson Mandela in 1994, every South African Prime Minister (or State President) was a member of the Broederbond. The effect of Broederbond membership on government, business and social life was immense.

With the tide of political change which swept through the country in the early 1990s, the Broederbond adopted a new constitution allowing women and other races to join, provided they all spoke Afrikaans. It then became known as the Afrikanerbond.

1936

The All-African National Convention drew together 400 delegates in Bloemfontein to oppose the '**Hertzog Bills**' which threatened to remove qualified Africans from the voters' roll. Despite widespread opposition, the **Representation of Natives (Blacks) Act of 1936** was passed in parliament, effectively disenfranchising the few African voters who had been on the voters' role in the Cape.

1936

Land allocated to the 'reserves' was doubled. It failed to improve the lot of those forced to subsist on land which was still insufficient and largely unsuitable for subsistence farming.

URBAN LIFE

Squatter camps and shanty towns developed in overcrowded black 'locations' as the black urban population rapidly increased. The 'locations' were characterised by their juxtaposition to spacious, leafy 'white' towns for which they supplied a source of cheap labour.

Inside the 'locations' or 'townships' (as they came to be known), a unique urban culture came into being. It was a culture which arose in direct response to conditions of repression and privation in African communities, and was marked by the heavy consumption of alcohol in 'shebeens' (informal pubs or taverns), gangsterism and sports, and the evolution of a distinctive popular music which derived from African traditional music fused with American ragtime and jazz, popularly known as *khwela*.

This culture was institutionalised by the so-called 'Drum School' of the 1950s. Journalists on **Drum Magazine** (such as Can Themba (1924 – 1968), Casey Motsisi (1932 – 1977) and Ben Nxumalo) found a genuine voice to express African aspirations, lifestyle and living conditions in the townships. From within the townships also, however, organised resistance started to emerge in the form of protests, stayaways and boycotts which would continue for the next 50 years.

1938

An Afrikaner nationalist organisation known as the **Ossewabrandwag** (Ox-wagon sentinels) was formed to commemorate the centenary of the Great Trek.

THE SECOND WORLD WAR (1939 – 1945)

When the Second World War broke out in 1939, pressure was again exerted on the Pact government for South Africa to enter the war on the British side. Hertzog, who was against this, and under considerable pressure, resigned as Prime Minister. Smuts, who had been requested by the Governor-General, Sir Patrick Duncan, to form a new government, then moved to put South African troops into active service for the allies against Germany. However, he did so with the outspoken opposition of Malan's HNP and on a slender majority of 80 to 67 when the vote was put to parliament.

Hertzog's resignation from the coalition made it possible for Malan to appropriate control of the National Party.

The war produced a boom in the manufacturing sectors of the economy which were said to produce as many as half the rifles and pistols used by the allies.

The extremist anti-war lobby, clustered mainly around the Ossewa-brandwag, openly supported Nazi Germany and embarked on a sabotage campaign at home. In 1942 hundreds of Brandwag members were arrested, among them **Balthazar Johannes Vorster** (1915 – 1983) who was later to become Prime Minister of the Republic of South Africa.

Deployed in northern Africa, Italy and in the campaign for Madagascar, South African troops of all races made a significant contribution to the war effort. With troops on various fronts, the people of Cape Town stopped for a short period of silence to remember soldiers in the war each day when the noon gun was fired from Signal Hill. Many militant Afrikaners refused to join this civil action and went on with their usual business during this time. Some even tried to prevent the periods of silence. The noon gun is still fired daily in Cape Town from Signal Hill.

The war had an important influence on the fight for democracy in this country. With black South Africans engaged in a fight for democracy and freedom in Europe, ANC leaders produced a document entitled 'African Claims' which emphasised the irony that these soldiers had no freedom and political rights at home.

1939 - 1945

Jock of the Bushveld was not the only famous canine in South African history. **'Just Nuisance, Able Seaman'** was enlisted in the Royal Navy at Simon's Town during the Second World War. The dog was a great morale booster for naval troops stationed at the base. On his death, he was buried with full military honours and is remembered today by his statue in Simon's Town.

1940

It was during the war that black protest in South Africa took a new lease on life. **Dr Alfred Xuma** (1893 – 1962) became president of the ANC and revived the organisation with a new administration and a membership drive. At this time the ANC continued to pursue moderate and petitionary forms of protest.

The **Non-European Unity Movement (NEUM)** led a pro-democracy campaign during the war years which involved boycotts and non-cooperation.

1943

The **United Party**, led by General Jan Smuts, won the election with 110 seats, as against the 43 of D F Malan's HNP.

1943

The **ANC Women's League** was reformed with Charlotte Maxeke as its first President. The League focused mainly on developing the anti-pass protest campaign.

1944

The **ANC Youth League** was formed spearheaded by Nelson Mandela (1918 –), Walter Sisulu (1912 – 2003), Oliver Tambo (1917 – 1993) and others. **Anton Muziwakhe Lembede** (1914 – 1947), an academic, teacher and lawyer, was elected the first leader of the youth league. They were more radical than the older members of the organisation, and wanted to project a strong message of African nationalism. The League issued a 'Programme of Action' setting out its proposals for a future non-racial and democratic South Africa, and advocating industrial action and mass civil disobedience as the strategy to bring about change. This marked a departure from the more moderate approach of Dr Xuma.

1946

The **African Mine Workers' Union** led a 100 000-strong miners' strike on the Rand, demanding a basic wage of 10 shillings a day. Seventy thousand black miners went on strike. Twelve miners were shot dead when state forces moved in to suppress the strike.

1946

The **Indian Passive Resistance Campaign** was launched by Yusuf Dadoo (1908 – 1983) and Dr G M Naicker. Backed by the ANC, the campaign aimed to mobilise action against the Asiatic Land Tenure and Indian Representation Acts introduced by the Smuts government.

1947

A **Congress Alliance**, bringing together the ANC and the Transvaal and Natal Indian Congresses, was forged.

From the beginning of the 20th century English and Afrikaner administrations in South Africa worked systematically towards building a system based entirely on discriminatory legislation and racist practice. At the end of the Second World War trends in European political thought tended towards putting the colonial past away and embracing, at least in theory, the ideas of autonomy, independence and integrity of all nations. A distortion of this notion was about to take hold in South Africa: a white state dominated by Afrikaner politicians was about to create an immensely powerful monolithic system of political control which promoted the idea of national self-determination only insofar as it served their interests of perpetuating white supremacy.

CHAPTER 7

THE RISE OF APARTHEID

1948 – 1960

This period marks the succession to power of the National Party, which had its origins in the Herenigde Nasionale Party started by Dr D F Malan in 1934. It followed a war which had deeply unsettled white South Africans, making them anxious about a future they saw as characterised by a 'native problem' and 'native militancy' which seemed to be on the increase. The National Party offered to deal with these problems. For many white South Africans, it appeared to be an inviting alternative to the United Party.

From its very beginnings the Afrikaner nationalist movement had embraced an ideology of racial purity, proclaiming the supremacy of the Afrikaner people over others. To boot, Afrikaners embraced a theology proclaiming that God had ordained this for his chosen people.

During these 12 years, before South Africa was proclaimed as a republic in 1961, almost 800 pieces of legislation were enacted – putting in place the legal infrastructure for the survival and growth of the apartheid system over the next 40 years.

Again the government introduced a programme of affirmative action to bring Afrikaans-speakers further into the burgeoning armed and civil services. For years to come Afrikaners dominated the army, navy and air force, as well as the railways, post office and all other public service quarters. Afrikaners therefore were not only the engineers of the apartheid system, but its public face also. English-speaking whites were by and large quiescent.

1948

In a close-run election, the **National Party** beat the United Party by the slender margin of only five seats and 39% of the vote. (Fewer votes were needed to win a parliamentary seat in the rural constituencies which were the mainstay of NP support.) After this election the demographic demarcation for voting was changed, giving even more power to rural areas, mainly inhabited by white Afrikaners. This resulted in the votes of a few hundred or thousand people in deep rural areas counting for as much as the votes of hundreds of thousands of people in urban areas, mainly the votes of English speakers. This ensured the National Party victory in forthcoming elections.

Dr D F Malan was inaugurated as Prime Minister and went on to form the new government which, like others before it, lacked legitimacy for the majority of the country's disenfranchised citizens.

Malan embarked on the **implementation of apartheid** which was a calculated legal separation of all the people in South Africa according to a hierarchy of race. Apartheid was not a new idea. It followed decades of European colonial and imperial rule in many parts of the world which had essentially regarded indigenes and people of a darker skin colour as inferior. Now the South African government implemented a coherent plan for rolling out race discriminatory legislation and gave it a brand-name: apartheid.

1949

The ANC, now headed by **Dr J S Moroka** (1891 –) as President and Walter Sisulu as Secretary, adopted the Youth League's **Programme of Action** which called for a stepping up of organised acts of civil disobedience and protest strikes. At this time also there was a move in the ANC to encourage a multi-racial (rather than exclusively African) political alliance to fight apartheid.

Implementing apartheid

1950

The **Population Registration Act of 1950** was one of the first pieces of apartheid legislation to be introduced. It classified all South Africans as either White, Coloured, Asiatic or Native. The 'native' category was subdivided into 10 groups, each defined by language. Coloured people were put into seven sub-groups ranging from Indian, Malay and Chinese to 'other Coloured'. Because the wording of this Act was inadequate and imprecise, sometimes individual members of the same family would be classified differently. Absurdities were often used by classifying officials to make a judgement about a person's race. One was the infamous '**pencil test**'. It involved sliding a pencil into a person's hair. If it remained there instead of slipping out, the person's hair was deemed too curly to be that of a white person.

The **Immorality Amendment Act of 1950** banned any sexual contact across colour lines and all inter-racial marriages. This extended Hertzog's 1927 ban on sex between blacks and whites. The Act brought humiliation and suffering to thousands, as families were broken up or declared unlawful. The Immorality Amendment Act allowed police to snoop on people's private lives, breaking up liaisons between whites and 'non-whites'. Invariably the punishment for the 'non-white' person would be considerably harsher.

THE GROUP AREAS ACT OF 1950

The Group Areas Act was the cornerstone of apartheid. It now was compulsory for all 'non-whites' to live only in areas especially segregated from white areas. The whole country was demarcated into separate areas for particular race groups and populations were moved en masse from one area to another. (For example: in 1966 the people of District Six were moved out of central Cape Town; in 1957 Indian people in Johannesburg were shipped out 40 kilometres to Lenasia; from 1958 to 1963 Cato Manor in Durban was cleared, with its residents being sent to the outskirts of the city – Umlazi, KwaMashu and Chatsworth; and in 1955 the Johannesburg suburb of Sophiatown was classified white, cleared at gun-point of its 60 000-strong black population and re-named 'Triomf'.)

During this time many people on the Rand were moved to **Soweto** (shortened from **So**uth **We**stern **To**wnships). Like many other townships, it was some considerable distance from the central business district of the town (in this case Johannesburg), making travel to and from work very expensive. With limited access routes, townships could be shut off from white towns abruptly in the event of civil unrest. Townships had very few facilities, and very small houses. Wide streets enabled enforcement agencies to patrol the streets.

It is estimated that more than 4 million people were forcibly moved under this legislation. Children especially suffered, with greatly increased deaths of infants and young children due to poverty and malnutrition. When people were moved, their houses were often destroyed, and they were dumped into strange areas without jobs, opportunities for work or any infrastructure, and the tight-knit communities that had previously supported them were destroyed.

The imposition of this Act was so thorough that an attempt was made to restrain one race from travelling through areas allocated to another race. So, for example, corridors of business and industry or green belts were created to ensure that blacks did not travel to and from work through white areas.

The Act had huge implications for all spheres of life in South Africa. Churches in the suburbs were no longer multi-racial, and although some people continued to travel long distances to worship in their old churches, it largely led to the separation of races in all areas of social activity.

1951

The **Suppression of Communism Act of 1951** allowed the Minister of Justice to outlaw any person or organisation viewed as 'communist'. Being communist in South Africa rapidly came to mean being opposed (in any way at all) to the apartheid government.

The **South African Censorship Board** became very active, banning books and magazines, including a copy of the *Daily Mirror* from Britain, which showed a black boxer having knocked out a white opponent. A Russian version of the book *The Fair House* by South African author Jack Cope was banned. The English version was freely available.

The **Bantu Authorities Act of 1951** took away the Representative Council established in 1936 when African male voters from the Cape were removed from the voters' roll. This council had very little power, but could advise government on certain issues. It was not widely supported.

By this stage the only 'legitimate' representatives of black people were the chiefs in the reserves, and there was no other form of representation in the decision-making of government.

1952

The **Natives Abolition of Passes and Coordination of Documents Act of 1952** did not abolish passes, but made them larger and more comprehensive. Black men were forced to carry these documents (commonly referred to as the

'dompas'), and were arrested and imprisoned if they were found without them. There was a difficult process to actually obtain a pass, and good reason for having one needed to be given. Enforcing the legislation consumed a huge amount of police energy and resources. It also kept people in a state of perpetual fear and anxiety as hundreds of thousands of people were prosecuted for infringements.

THE SEPARATE AMENITIES ACT OF 1953

The Separate Amenities Act designated all parks, libraries, zoos, beaches and public places in general to various race groups. The bulk of the amenities in urban areas, including beaches, were designated for 'white' use.

A curious inconsistency was that for many years, one had to enter the post office by a different door and be attended to at a different counter (according to your race group) and yet the banks were integrated – with the various race groups queuing together for service.

As with the Group Areas Act, this legislation was expensive to implement. It required the building of separate hospitals, libraries, post office facilities, hotels, and public toilets. Needless to say the facilities provided for groups other than whites were inadequate.

Even public parks were dedicated to a single race, with benches clearly marked 'whites only' or 'non-whites only'. Examples of these can be seen today at the Apartheid Museum in southern Johannesburg.

These policies gave apartheid a very public face and caused widespread resentment and anger. The policy was so extreme that if borrowers at a public library had their domestic workers return books, they were asked to wrap the books to ensure they were kept clean.

1953

The **Bantu Education Act of 1953** moved control of African schools from the provinces to a central Bantu Education Department headed by **Dr Hendrik Verwoerd** (1901 – 1966) whose stipulated aim was for black people to be educated only 'in accordance with their opportunities in life'. Essentially it sought to deliver a servile and obedient labour force for exploitation in the industrial sector.

By reducing or eliminating state subsidies, the Act forced the closure of many mission schools. One of those to close was **Tiger Kloof School** in the Vryburg area of the western Transvaal which had educated several Botswanan political figures. These schools had been a mainstay of education for 70% of the black community.

In the words of Verwoerd:

[1]*"The Natives will be taught from childhood to realise that equality with Europeans is not for them. There is no place for the Bantu child above the level of certain forms of labour. Until now, he has been subjected to a school system which drew him away from his own community and misled him by showing him the green pastures of European society in which he was not allowed to graze."*[1]

With the introduction of apartheid legislation, attacks on individuals and communities became commonplace. Black informal traders and small business entrepreneurs were forced out of urban and white areas, or driven out of business altogether. Townships were frequently raided and shebeen-owners arrested and prosecuted under laws regulating the sale of liquor to Africans.

The apartheid laws were felt in the workplace, in churches, in schools, in sports – in short, in every sphere of life in South Africa.

A number of trade unions, realising the strength of unity, started to organise unions comprising all the race groups. The government soon put a stop to this by introducing legislation banning multi-racial trade unions. They still refused to recognise black-only unions. The *Cape Times* quoted Senator J de Klerk, Minister of Labour, as saying that there were places of work where coloured journeymen were training European apprentices. "This can no longer be tolerated, because it imperils European civilisation."

It is difficult to pronounce on which of the apartheid laws was the most debilitating and humiliating for the African majority. Each compounded the one before it. In the words of Nelson Mandela, apartheid was ...

[1] Quoted in Mason, David: *South Africa*, p. 176

[1]*"...the codification in one oppressive system of all the laws and regulations that had kept African in an inferior position to whites for centuries ... The often haphazard segregation of the past three hundred years was to be consolidated into a monolithic system that was diabolical in its detail, inescapable in its reach and overwhelming in its power."* [ii]

Protest

1950s

The introduction of apartheid legislation brought a massive increase in acts of **civil disobedience** and protest. On 1 May 1950 the Communist Party in Johannesburg organised a stayaway to protest against low wages, against government plans to ban the party, and against political repression in general. Police fired into the crowds, killing 18 people.

Nelson Mandela claimed that this day was a turning point in his life, when he understood how far the police were prepared to go, and how ruthlessly they were prepared to stand against any sort of defiance campaign to maintain the status quo.

On 26 June a National Day of Protest and Mourning was called by the ANC in protest at the police shootings. Large numbers of workers from across the racial spectrum were involved in protests on this day, laying the foundations for a nationwide anti-apartheid alliance.

THE DEFIANCE CAMPAIGN

The 1952 Defiance Campaign led jointly by the Communist Party and the ANC – now under the leadership of **Albert Luthuli** (1898 – 1967) – aimed to draw attention and offer passive resistance to the welter of unjust laws. Inspired by the Gandhian idea of passive resistance, the campaign got off the ground at the same time as many white South Africans were celebrating the tercentenary of the 1652 arrival in the Cape of Jan van Riebeeck.

The campaign took the form of mass marches through cities, pass burning and the flouting of 'petty apartheid' laws through the occupation of areas reserved for whites only. While the protests were for the most part

[i] Mandela, Nelson: *Long Walk To Freedom*, p. 127

peaceful in nature, police often provoked crowds into riotous behaviour resulting in some incidents of looting and the destruction of property.

Up to 8 000 activists were arrested for their involvement in the Defiance Campaign. Their leaders were convicted under the Suppression of Communism Act and the campaign was crushed. However, it had put the question of the legitimacy of the apartheid state squarely on the international agenda.

Although the modis operandi of the campaign was 'peaceful', it was called off after three months, after many violent incidents and the arrest of its leaders, including President Luthuli and Secretary-General Sisulu, under the Suppression of Communism Act. The government's ruthless dealing with the campaign had been applauded by the white electorate in spite of the fact that the whole exercise had catapulted the South African struggle onto the world stage and had brought a massive increase in membership numbers of the ANC.

1953

The non-racial **Liberal Party of South Africa** was formed with the aim of bringing about a non-racial society in South Africa, based on the electoral principle of 'one man one vote'. The Liberal Party was opposed to all forms of totalitarianism and vehemently opposed to the oppressive and unjust system of apartheid. It tended to attract middle-class and academic whites to its membership, though it claimed as members a good many African people in rural areas.

1954

The **Federation of South African Women (FEDSAW)** was formed on 17 April with Ida Mntwana as President and Ray Alexander as National Secretary.

Influential writer **Alan Paton** (1903 – 1988) published *Cry the Beloved Country* to international acclaim. The novel played an important role in depicting conditions in South Africa for the public in both Britain and America.

1955

The **South African Congress of Trade Unions (SACTU)** was formed. This was the first non-racial trade union organisation in South Africa.

The **Congress Alliance** was also created drawing together all race groups, left-wing organisations and activists working for change.

It received support from the United Nations, who had, by this time, recognised the human rights violations taking place in the name of apartheid.

FREEDOM CHARTER

At a 3 000-strong meeting of the Congress of the People on 25 June at Kliptown near Johannesburg, the **Freedom Charter** was signed and adopted as a strategy for change and a vision for post-apartheid South Africa. The meeting, which was the most representative gathering ever held in South Africa at that time, was interrupted by the police who searched and interrogated delegates while Congress business proceeded. The Charter stated:

> The People shall govern!
> All national groups shall have equal rights!
> People shall share in the country's wealth!
> The land shall be shared among those who work it!
> All shall be equal before the law!
> All shall enjoy equal human rights!
> There shall be work and security!
> The doors of learning and of culture shall be opened!
> There shall be houses, security and comfort!
> There shall be peace and friendship!

It ended with a call to action:

These freedoms we will fight for, side by side, throughout our lives, until we have won our victory.

THE BLACK SASH

The Black Sash was formed in 1955 when six white Johannesburg-based women met at a tea party and discussed their opposition to the Senate Bill which called for a two-thirds majority of both houses of parliament to remove coloureds from the voters' roll. The organisation grew rapidly, becoming a forum for liberal white women to oppose government policies and the enforcement of apartheid legislation.

A Black Sash draped over the constitution became the symbolic representation for their mourning over the corrupted constitution. The organisation came to be known as the Black Sash for this symbol and by the sash which members wore, draped over the right shoulder, during protests.

Black Sash protests took the form of silent public 'stands', marches, convoys, demonstrations and vigils. Individual members were subjected to state harassment and detention as the struggle against apartheid intensified over the next 35 years.

In the beginning, the Black Sash was concerned with monitoring pass law courts to expose the injustices inherent in the pass law system. They set up Advice Offices in various parts of the country to deal these and related civil rights abuses. After the 1994 elections, the Black Sash shifted focus from being a protest organisation to become a professional one, still upholding the same principles in making submissions to government to shape welfare-related legislation.

1956

The **Tomlinson Commission** was asked to look at improving the economic development of the 'Bantu' reserves, with the intention that development would discourage migration into towns and cities. Their recommendations were rejected by government as being too costly, and they were not willing to increase the size of the reserve areas dedicated to black settlement. However, the report did pave the way for turning reserves into 'homelands'.

WOMEN STRIKE AGAINST APARTHEID

Women became particularly prominent in resistance to apartheid. Many lived in poverty in the reserves and brought up children threatened with malnutrition, illness and high levels of infant and child mortality. Many left their own families to seek poor-paying jobs in domestic service in white homes. Some women found temporary work on white farms. Others joined the industrial work force. **FEDSAW** led a number of peaceful, mass demonstrations to highlight the plight of African women, predominantly with respect to the pass laws.

In August 1956, 20 000 women, led by ANC Women's League President, **Lilian Ngoyi** (1911 – 1980), **Helen Joseph** (1905 – 1992), Sophie Williams and Rahima Moosa, marched peacefully to the Union Buildings in Pretoria singing *Nkosi Sikelel'i Afrika* and chanting *'Wathint'abafazi, wathint'* *'imbokodo, Uzakufa'* ('You have tampered with the women! You have struck a rock! You will be crushed!') to protest against being forced to carry pass books. The leaders were refused entry to the office of the Prime Minister, J G Strijdom (1893 – 1958).

It was the largest political gathering of women to date. While the march had enormous symbolic significance, ultimately it failed to make an impression. Pass-law restrictions were extended to women in the early 1960s, and restricted the rights of black women without steady employment to stay in urban areas for longer than 72 hours. South Africa still celebrates Women's Day on 9 August each year, to remember this march.

In 1956 **Trevor Huddlestone** (a priest from the Community of the Resurrection in Johannesburg) published *Nought for your Comfort*, detailing his experiences in Sophiatown in a powerful indictment of the apartheid system.

SOPHIATOWN

Situated west of Johannesburg, Sophiatown was a vibrant community of artists, musicians, writers and others who gave urban black culture a distinct voice and a powerful cultural identity. An indigenous brand of urban music styles evolved in townships like Sophiatown combining kwela, marabi and American jazz.

Under the Group Areas Act, Sophiatown was razed to the ground and given over to whites who named the new suburb Triomf (Triumph). Sophiatown residents mounted a brave campaign to halt the removals in the late 1950s. They were ultimately unsuccessful, and many were forcibly removed to Meadowlands in Soweto.

1956

In December, in response to the launching of the Freedom Charter the year before, the government arrested 156 Congress leaders, including Walter Sisulu and Nelson Mandela, and charged them with treason. State prosecutors claimed that the Charter intended to incite violence as a means to bring down the state. The trialists themselves claimed they were fighting for basic human rights, including the right to organise and participate in political and economic activities.

Of the 156 people originally arrested, 91 were actually brought to trial. The **Treason Trial** dragged on for five years before it collapsed and the defendants were cleared. Many of the trialists were then banned to prevent them being able to lead.

1956

The **Senate Act** was passed, removing coloured males from the voters' roll. From this time, until 1983, the only people who had the right to vote in South Africa were those classified as belonging to the white race group.

1957

Urban protests against pass controls, rising prices, poor living conditions, the lack of job opportunities and police harassment were gathering momentum. In Alexandra township a **bus boycott** was launched to protest hikes in bus fares.

Thousands of residents walked 20 kilometres to work and back. It was followed by the 'pound-a-day' national minimum wage campaign. These and other campaigns enjoyed a measure of success, particularly in effecting mass stayaway from work. However, most protest collapsed due to economic necessity and official harassment.

In the impoverished rural areas, protests took the form of **tax boycotts** and pressure began to be exerted on tax collectors, government agents and state-appointed chiefs who were seen as no better than state stooges.

In this year the National Party government adopted **Die Stem van Suid-Afrika** (The Call of South Africa) as its national anthem.

1958

Hendrik Verwoerd assumed leadership of the government. Verwoerd was widely seen as the mastermind of apartheid which he described as a policy of 'good neighbourliness'. He enjoyed great popularity with the electorate, promising to protect white agricultural and industrial interests and to move South Africa towards a political break with Britain. Verwoerd's regime came to be distinguished for its 'verkrampte' (hard-line) approach to the administration of apartheid. He ruthlessly crushed opposition and through strict laws of censorship, took steps to prevent the infiltration of liberal or radical ideas emanating from abroad. South Africa was increasingly isolated from the world community.

1959

An Africanist group led by **Robert Sobukwe** (1924 – 1978) and Potlako Leballo (d. 1963) were frustrated by the multi-racial aspects of the resistance movement and wanted a more forceful outlet for the anger of the people. They broke away from the ANC structures to form the **Pan Africanist Congress (PAC)**. The PAC determined that ANC policies were insufficiently radical to initiate change, and they began to mobilise people, especially in the Cape and southern Vaal townships, against the government.

The **Extension of University Education Act of 1959** denied black students the opportunity to attend the universities of their choice, and led to the formation of separate colleges for the various ethnic groups. These new universities included the University of the Western Cape for coloureds, the University of Durban-Westville for Indians, the University of the North for Sesotho and Setswana speakers, the University of Zululand for isiZulu speakers, and the University of Fort Hare for isiXhosa speakers.

1959

In June 1959 there was a violent riot in Mkhumbane (**Cato Manor**, Durban) when women protested against police raids on shebeens and forced removals to KwaMashu and Umlazi under the Group Areas Act. Many of the women relied on the shebeens (where they sold home brewed liquor) for their livelihoods.

The protests and police response to them only increased in intensity. In January 1960, nine policemen were murdered by angry residents of Mkhumbane during a liquor raid.

Eight 'Bantustans' or '**homelands**' came into being, to be administered by local chiefs appointed by the government. The homelands were created along ethnic and linguistic lines, each forming an 'autonomous' nation. This now meant that Africans were effectively denied their right to South African citizenship. The Promotion of Bantu Self-Government Act of 1959 made provision for the eventual transformation of the homelands into independent states.

The largest revolt against the proposed homeland system at this time took place in Pondoland.

THE PONDOLAND REVOLT

In the late 1950s, ANC supporters referring to themselves as 'iKongi' (Congress supporters) rose up in revolt against the imposition of tribal authorities and impending self-government for the homeland of Transkei. The revolt was marked by a number of incidents of violence involving iKongi members and the security forces. Local chiefs and other people regarded as 'collaborators' with the government were targeted for attack. At least eight chiefs and their councillors were killed and their huts burned.

The revolt was crushed by the security forces and thousands of iKongi members were detained and tortured while in custody. Seventeen people were killed, some in police custody, others through the security forces' use of unnecessary force in public order policing. This was a practice which would become commonplace in the 30 years of resistance which lay ahead.

By the end of the 1950s, the Nationalist government was firmly entrenched in power. All that remained was for it to finally sever ties with Britain. This was accomplished in the next few years.

The 1960s would see Britain handing over its naval base of Simon's Town to the Union and the abolition of all symbols and insignia associated with the former British empire. A new South African flag was unfurled and *God Save the Queen* gave way to *Die Stem*.

Opposition to apartheid was equally established. However, the resistance movement in this country was about to enter its darkest period yet as security forces were increased and given more capacity and resources to deal with protest and insurrection.

CHAPTER 8

SHARPEVILLE AND AFTER

1960 – 1980

The Sharpeville massacre in 1960 marked a turning point in South African history. For the first time the government invoked the Public Safety Act of 1953 to call a state of emergency to quell an uprising which had ripples throughout the country. The event drew heavy condemnation from the international community. Far from backing down, the government instead sought to crush resistance with greater might than ever before. It used the Unlawful Organisations Act of 1960 to ban the ANC and the PAC. As avenues for peaceful political protest closed down, the ANC and PAC opted to take up arms in the ongoing struggle for political equality. A cycle of violence and counter-violence began and escalated over the next 30 years.

1960

The year opened with a catastrophic mining disaster at **Clydesdale colliery** when a mine collapsed trapping 440 miners. There were no survivors.

THE SHARPEVILLE MASSACRE

On 21 March 1960, police opened fire on a 5 000-strong unarmed crowd during a protest against pass laws in Sharpeville, near Vereeniging. Sixty-nine civilian protesters were killed, eight of them women and ten children, and 180 people were wounded. Gunshot wounds indicated that most of them had been shot while fleeing from the police.

The march at Sharpeville had been organised primarily by the PAC. It led to the banning of the ANC and PAC on 8 April and the announcement of a state of emergency in nearly half of the magisterial districts of the country. New security legislation gave the police powers of arrest without the necessity of taking people to court. In 1962 the police could detain people for 12 days without trial. This was increased to 90 days by 1963, and 180 days in 1965. By 1967 detention could be for any length of time.

Thousands of ANC, SACP (South African Communist Party) and PAC members were arrested and detained without trial. Oliver Tambo and several other leaders managed to escape through neighbouring states. Now banned at home, the ANC and PAC moved to establish bases in Tanzania.

The shooting provoked widespread international outrage. This was largely ignored by the government. Attempts were made by the United Nations to impose serious economic sanctions on the South African government. Although British and American interests prevented this from happening, there was some withdrawal of foreign capital from South Africa for a time.

Having reached the conclusion that non-violent methods of protest were largely ineffective, many African activists started to formulate a policy of using more direct tactics to oppose the regime. Nelson Mandela wrote:

"The time comes in the life of any nation where there remain only two choices: submit or fight. That time has now come to South Africa. We shall not submit and we have no choice but to hit back by all means within our power in defence of our people, our future and our freedom."

Days after the Sharpeville massacre, two people were killed and 47 wounded in **Langa**, Cape Town, when police opened fire on a crowd of anti-pass protestors.

As a response to this massacre, the ANC called for a stayaway on 28 March. Most African workers stayed away from work on this day.

In a climate of conflict and heavy-handed media controls, urban legends started doing the rounds after the Sharpeville killings. One held that several days were to be set aside by blacks to kill white people. These dates included 28 March 1960 and 31 May 1961. In response to these legends, thousands of white men and women armed themselves with handguns. (The 'Kill-a-White-Day' rumour raised its head again after the unbanning of the ANC and SACP in February 1990. The day set aside was said to be 10 April 1990.)

1960

British Prime Minister, Harold Macmillan (1894 – 1986) made his famous '**Wind of Change**' address in parliament in Cape Town. In it came the warning that colonial rule had become increasingly untenable and unsustainable. The British government now believed that political and economic development in society should rest on individual merit, regardless of skin colour. The speech infuriated the apartheid government.

1960

In October, just months after the Sharpeville massacre, a **referendum** was held to decide whether the Union of South Africa should become a republic. Only white South Africans were allowed to vote, and of the 1.6 million people who voted, 52% supported the move to become a republic. Thus, once more, the fate of the country was changed through a small majority of votes of a small minority of the population. The National Party government declared South Africa a republic. The move held enormous symbolic significance for Afrikaners who felt that they had finally severed ties with an imperial nation against which they had struggled for 200 years.

Throughout the 60s, apartheid reached even more ridiculous levels. New subways were built at several stations in the Cape peninsula, including one at Salt River where commuting black and white workers could access platforms through different subways although they were headed for a day's work in the same workshop.

The railway authorities decided that Fish Hoek also needed a new subway as the existing one was not wide enough to have a hand rail in the centre separating the races.

Kokstad went even further. There were three entrances to the post office marked: 'Europeans', 'Non-Europeans except Natives', and 'Natives'.

At the time the honourable Minister of Agricultural Technical Services, P le Roux stated:

"There is no country in the world, except South Africa, where the Whites have governed a non-White people without exploiting and impoverishing them."

On another tack, the *Sunday Times* reported that an African child had been found to be wearing a blazer from Tzaneen Primary School. The blazer was taken from him in exchange for two pullovers, and was burned in front of the whole school assembly to show the children that giving school garments to 'natives' was unsuitable behaviour.

Bloemfontein decreed that the vegetable market would be open to whites until 9.30 am, thereafter 'non-whites' would be allowed in to buy.

The Argus reported that the Minister of Education (Senator J de Klerk – father of the later President F W de Klerk) ordered that all scientific bodies be reserved for whites, and that 'non-whites' be excluded. He sent a special reminder to the South African Bird Watchers in May 1964 to ask whether they had implemented this policy.

1961

On 31 May, South Africa became an **independent republic**.

South Africa left the British Commonwealth following harsh censure by leading member states. The referendum had endorsed this move. However, it stemmed also from the United Nations declaration that the policy of apartheid was a crime against humanity.

1961

In the General Elections, the Nationalist Party increased their majority and won 105 of the 160 seats in Parliament.

At this time the South African Rand was decimalised. People with long memories may remember the jingle on the radio:

"Decimal Dan, the Rand Cent man
Gives you cents for pennies whenever he can
One cent for a penny, and two for two
And two and a half for a tiekie[1].
The notes and silver are just the same
Except that there's a change in their name."

[1] A tiekie was a small coin, equal to the British three-penny bit ($2\frac{1}{2}$ cents)

1961

Chief Albert Luthuli won worldwide acclaim when he was awarded the **Nobel Peace Prize** in December 1961. Albert Luthuli was a chief in the Groutville district of Natal. He was sacked as chief after he came out in support of the Defiance Campaign. He was banned by the government, but nevertheless led the ANC as President General until his death in July 1967. He was hit by a train while crossing a railway line.

THE ARMED STRUGGLE

The ANC elected to embark on an underground armed struggle. **Umkhonto weSizwe** (MK/the 'Spear of the Nation') was launched on 16 December (then 'Dingaan's Day') as the separate military wing of the ANC. It was important that this military wing was outside primary ANC structures, and its objective was to destroy government property in a campaign of sabotage. A founding principle was to avoid bloodshed as far as possible. For half a century the ANC had embraced the core principle of non-violence. The decision to adopt an armed struggle was not an easy one.

Over the next year and a half, more than 200 targets around the country were attacked by MK operatives. These were mainly power lines, railway lines and public buildings. Some undisciplined operatives also attacked the homes of police and other 'soft' targets.

A radical white organisation, the National Committee of Liberation, also engaged in a bombing campaign in central Johannesburg and Cape Town.

In September 1961 the PAC formed an armed wing, uPoqo (meaning 'pure') whose objective was to stimulate a general black uprising through military provocation. While this objective was not achieved, the uPoqo campaign carried out indiscriminate attacks on the police, government agents, suspected police informers and whites. In a crackdown on the organisation, more than 3000 members were detained.

1962

Government reaction to the emerging **underground resistance** campaign was fierce. The security forces were successful in infiltrating many underground cells. Underground leaders were pursued and arrested if they had not been driven into exile abroad. Nelson Mandela managed to leave the country

secretly and travel over much of Africa and Britain to gain support for the ANC and the struggle. Dubbed 'The Black Pimpernel', he managed to live clandestinely for over a year before he was caught near Howick in Natal in August 1962 and sentenced to five years' in jail for organising the May 1961 stayaway, and for leaving the country without a passport.

1963

The **General Law Amendment Act of 1961** authorised the police to detain people without access to a lawyer for 90 days. Frequently, detainees would be released after 90 days and immediately re-arrested. Allegations of torture and deaths in detention soon followed. PAC member Bellington Mampe (1933 – 1963) and ANC supporters Looksmart Ngudle (d.1963) and Suliman Saloojee (d.1964) all died after being tortured in detention. By 1970, some 22 people had met their **deaths in detention** for similar reasons. Police routinely offered causes of death such as 'fell out of a window', 'slipped on soap in shower' or 'suicide by hanging' and these excuses were frequently accepted by inquest courts.

In June 1963, an intelligence wing was established in the police. This later became the Bureau of State Security (BOSS).

In this year Indians were recognised as South African citizens for the first time, and in the late 1960s the government set up the **South African Indian Council**. This had very little support from Indians and was largely ignored.

The strange elements of apartheid multiplied: The Cape Times reported that in Beaufort West it was decided that non-white drama and theatre groups could give performances in the Town Hall, but these performances could only be attended by white people.

This became a common practice. When the Nico Malan Theatre opened on the Foreshore in Cape Town, no 'non-whites' were allowed to either perform or attend performances. This excluded the very accomplished 'Eon Group', and many white Cape Town theatre goers boycotted the theatre for years as a result.

THE RIVONIA TRIAL

Most of the underground ANC leadership were arrested in July 1963 at the movement's secret headquarters on the farm '**Lilliesleaf**' at Rivonia outside Johannesburg in July 1963. They were tried on charges of sabotage and attempting to overthrow the government and in 1964 eight were sentenced to life imprisonment. These were Nelson Mandela, Govan Mbeki (1910 – 2001), Walter Sisulu, Raymond Mhlaba, Andrew Mlangeni, Elias Motsoaledi, Ahmed Kathrada, and Denis Goldberg. All (except Goldberg) were sent to Robben Island to begin their sentences.

During the trial, Mandela (already serving a sentence for having left the country illegally) addressed the court, saying:

"It is a struggle for the right to live. During my lifetime I have dedicated myself to this struggle of the African people. I have fought against White domination, and I have fought against Black domination. I have cherished the ideal of a democratic and free society in which all persons live together in harmony and with equal opportunities. It is an ideal which I hope to live for and to achieve. But if needs be, it is an ideal for which I am prepared to die."

On his release from prison 26 years later, Mandela used the same words to greet the tens of thousands of people who had gathered at the Grand Parade in Cape Town to welcome him.

Later, a worldwide campaign for the release of political prisoners, and Mandela especially, would become a mobilising factor for the anti-apartheid struggle.

Chief Albert Luthuli made a statement about the trialists:

"They are sentenced to be shut away for long years in the brutal and degrading prisons of South Africa. With them will be interred the country's hopes for racial co-operation. They will leave a vacuum in leadership that may only be filled by bitter hate and racial strife."

Following the trial, the ANC, headed now by Oliver Tambo, consolidated its headquarters in exile – with a presence in London, Dar-es-Salaam and Lusaka.

1963

The policy of 'Bantu self-government' first legislated in 1959 was effected in 1963 when the **Transkei** homeland administration came into being. It was headed by Chief Kaizer Matanzima who had seen fit to say about the home-lands scheme (in the *Cape Times* on 28 August) that: "To me, separate development is what Magna Carta[1] is to the people of Britain".

Bophuthatswana, Venda and Ciskei were each granted 'self-governing status' and installed with homeland assemblies in the 70s, and like the Transkei before them, each developed the symbols of statehood in a special anthem and a special flag. Each was wholly dependent on South Africa for budgetary and security requirements. Homeland officials were singled out as 'collaborators' and lost authority and influence. Some became vulnerable to attack. Nowhere in the world, other than in South Africa, was their official status recognised.

RESISTANCE AGAINST THE HOMELANDS

Even aside from the ANC, SACP and PAC, most African people were against the homeland reserves. The government's policy succeeded, however, with the participation of some chiefs and others who took up bureaucratic posi-tions in the administrations, and the participation of black businessmen who gained from having no white competition.

During the 1960s and early 1970s over three million people were moved from 'white' South Africa to resettlement areas in the homelands – barren, isolated land where they faced extreme poverty. A lack of basic amenities and job opportunities to support local populations precipitated a massive health crisis, particularly in children, many of whom suffered from kwashiorkor, a condition caused by malnutrition.

Men and women travelled to the cities to look for work, leaving their families behind. Many men took up with other women in the urban areas, and soon forgot their families in the Bantustans, leaving them to fend for themselves or starve.

One of the Nationalist ministers of the time, H J Botha, expressed his opinion on the homeland policy saying in the House of Assembly that his forefathers had built dykes in Zeeland to keep out the North Sea; the Afrikaners today were constructing traditional dykes around South Africa to keep out the black hordes.

[1] The Magna Carta was signed in Britain in 1215 to define the obligations of the barons to the monarch, and to confirm the liberties of the Church of England.

1964

John Harris (d.1965), a member of a radical white organisation, the **African Resistance Movement**, detonated a bomb in Johannesburg station, killing one person and injuring 22 others. Harris was later given the death sentence and executed for this action.

1965

The **Criminal Procedure Amendment Act of 1965** now empowered the police to detain people for 180 days with the possibility of re-detention thereafter. Detainees could be held in solitary confinement for six months with only state officials permitted access to them.

Bram Fischer (1926 – 1975), a senior advocate and grandson of a former OFS President, was arrested with 14 others in August 1964 and charged with furthering the aims of the SACP. In 1965 all were sentenced to terms of imprisonment. Fischer was given a life sentence. He was diagnosed with cancer in the early 70s and died at home having been released a few days earlier.

1965

In neighbouring **Rhodesia, Prime Minister Ian Smith** declared a Unilateral Declaration of Independence (UDI) from Britain. Many years of civil war followed before Zimbabwe finally attained its independence under the leadership of Robert Mugabe in 1980.

1966

In September 1966 **Prime Minister Hendrik Verwoerd** was murdered in parliament by **Dimitri Tsafendas** who was alleged to be mentally ill. Tsafendas spent the rest of his life in prison and mental institutions until he died in the late 1990s. Early in his premiership (in 1960), Verwoerd had survived another assassination attempt when he was shot in the head by a deranged white farmer. **Balthazar Johannes ('BJ') Vorster** (1915 – 1983) succeeded Verwoerd as prime minister.

South African security forces clashed with **SWAPO** troops in northern South-West-Africa, starting a war which lasted for 23 years.

1967

Military service was made compulsory for all white males who had hitherto been conscripted through a ballot system. This was initiated by P W Botha (1916 – 2006), who had been made Minister of Defence in 1966.

Oliver Tambo took over leadership of the ANC on the death of Albert Luthuli.

A new military wing for the PAC was established in the form of the **Azanian People's Liberation Army (APLA).**

Professor Chris Barnard performed the world's first heart transplant on a dentist, Dr Louis Washkansky on 3 December 1967. The transplant could have taken place two weeks earlier if a coloured donor had been acceptable. The transplant team, however, decided that no inter-racial transplants would take place as it would be out of place in the apartheid system to put a black donor organ into a white person, or vice-versa.

In this year also the first **Krugerrand**, South Africa's gold coin which became a worldwide collector's item, was minted. South Africa has since produced over 50 000 gold Krugerrands.

In this year the non-racial **Liberal Party of South Africa** was forced to disband with the government's passing of the Prohibition of Improper Interference Act, which made non-racial parties illegal. Many of its members had experienced detention and banning in the 15 years since its inception in 1953.

The **Bureau of State Security (BOSS)** started to function outside the police force, directly accountable to Prime Minister B J Vorster. Heavily funded by the state, its activities were shrouded in secrecy. It went on to undertake both internal and external security 'operations' involving espionage as well as direct attacks on individuals and organisations, going some way to transforming South Africa into a police state during the 70s.

By this time the pass laws were being very strictly implemented. Nearly one million people were arrested during this year – nearly 2 000 per day. Hundreds of thousands of people were forced to go to rural areas. Men in towns were forced to live in single-sex hostels away from their families. Men who wanted to work

in the cities had to go through a gruelling and humiliating medical examination including examination of their genitals to ensure they had no disease.

A large amount of security force energies were concentrated on efforts to maintain 'separate development', such as seeing that people did not socialise or attend functions together. Police activities were concentrated in the 'white' areas, and crime began to rage in the townships due to lack of policing and poor social conditions. The repercussions of this policy live with us today.

The government set up a **Coloured Persons Representative Council** which had no real powers and was not supported by the coloured people.

1969

At the first **ANC consultative conference** in Morogoro, Tanzania, the 'Strategies and Tactics' programme was adopted, introducing a fresh approach to armed struggle and political mobilisation. ANC leaders decided to allow all race groups to join the organisation as full members. The ANC had made alliances outside the country and many ANC members were receiving training in other countries in Africa, in Russia and in Cuba. While the ANC in exile was very strong, the PAC in exile was by this time threatened with internal conflict.

Also in this year the **South African Students' Organisation (SASO)** was founded by Steve Bantu Biko (1942 – 1977), Barney Pityana and others who began to promote the ideology of **black consciousness**. Arguing that blacks were held back by white liberalism and paternalism, black consciousness leaders advocated a black separatism and promoted the idea of self-pride for blacks as the only way to achieve psychological liberation.

Conditions in South African **mines** were still extremely unsafe, and workers still risked their lives to mine gold. An explosion at **Buffelsfontein** killed 62 miners and injured another 29.

The **international sanction on sports** was beginning to take effect. Having been expelled from the International Olympic Committee in 1968, white South Africans were beginning to feel their isolation in the worldwide cricket and rugby fraternities with public demonstrations against apartheid attending most international fixtures. However, rebel tours at home and abroad continued drawing the Springboks more and more into the glare of publicity.

RESISTANCE IN THE 1970s

Anti-apartheid protests among the intelligentsia grew apace during the 1970s roping in writers, students, lawyers, economists, historians, social scientists and theologians. While the churches were never fully united in the anti-apartheid struggle, many (barring the Dutch Reformed Church) started to advocate a theology of liberation to expose the hypocrisy and inhumanity of apartheid.

In a move which angered white South Africa, the World Council of Churches allocated R91 000 of its annual R140 000 fund against racism to liberation movements in southern Africa – including SWAPO, the ANC and anti-apartheid groups.

Student revolts in Europe and the USA during these years encouraged South African students in their militancy. American students had protested against participation in the Vietnam War. In South Africa students fought against apartheid and in white universities against military conscription which, in 1972, was extended from nine to 12 months with a 19-day annual call-up for five years. Many student activists found a political home in the National Union of South African Students (NUSAS) which had been in existence for some decades.

Student protests were gathering momentum. Many were broken up by the police. In 1972 students organised a protest meeting at the top of Wale Street in Cape Town. Police baton-charged protesters, resulting in several injuries. During the following year the student leadership was banned, including eight leaders of SASO.

1972

The **Black People's Convention (BPC)** was launched as an umbrella body to co-ordinate black consciousness groups.

The government appointed a commission of enquiry (the **Schlebush Commission**) to investigate the activities of several anti-apartheid bodies including the University Christian Movement (UCM), NUSAS, the Christian Institute of Southern Africa, the South African Institute of Race Relations, and other related organisations. Inevitably it led to the curtailing of their work.

THE AFRIKANER WEERSTANDSBEWEGING (AWB)

The Afrikaner Weerstandsbeweging (Afrikaner Resistance Movement) was founded in Heidelberg during 1973 on a radical right-wing manifesto. Headed by **Eugene Terre'Blanche** (1941 –), who felt the government of B J Vorster was going 'soft' on race, the AWB was started as a cultural/political movement with the aim of protecting the interests of Afrikaners, uniting the boerevolk (Boer people) and establishing a volkstaat (nation-state) similar in form to the old Boer republics. The AWB was not willing to further its cause at the ballot box or negotiating table. Terre'Blanche stated on numerous occasions that the borders of such a volkstaat would be drawn in blood. Later the AWB took up arms to further its political interests.

1973

Against the backdrop of a world depression, a **wave of strikes** broke out on the Rand and in Natal. As many as 60 000 workers downed tools in protest against the cutting of wages and redundancies. This stimulated the growth of the trade union movement.

In response to the oil crisis, the **speed limit** in South Africa was reduced from 120 kph to 80 kph. This led to a massive decrease in fatalities – a clear indication of the truth of the statement 'speed kills'. Following an African and Arab embargo on oil, petrol was sold only during daylight hours. Various other fuel restrictions were imposed including a ban on carrying petrol in cans.

1974

The **Metal and Allied Workers' Union** was established.

The United Nations withdrew the credentials of the South African delegation. The ANC and PAC were granted observer status.

In this year also SASO founder **Ongkopotse Abraham Tiro** was killed by a parcel bomb in Botswana, and **Boy Mvemve** (John Dube) was killed by a letter bomb in Zambia. These represent the first 'cross border' operations by the security forces.

Rallies in support of the Mozambican liberation organisation, FRELIMO, were held in Durban and at the University of the North. After the protests were broken up by the police, many BPC and SASO leaders were detained and tortured.

1975

Chief **Mangosuthu Buthelezi** (1928 –) revived the cultural movement called '**Inkatha**' which was first established in the 1920s. This organisation (later to become a political party – the Inkatha Freedom Party/IFP) initially had close ties with the ANC although it had a predominantly Zulu-nationalist political identity.

In this year **Mozambique** and **Angola** gained independence from Portugal. Through its support for rebel movements, RENAMO (in Mozambique) and UNITA (in Angola), South Africa continued to conduct destabilising operations in both countries, refusing to recognise their independent governments. Conflict in Angola developed into a full-scale civil war which continued for 13 years.

1976

Transkei was granted 'independence' from South Africa. About this event, Defence Minister P W Botha stated in the House of Assembly: "*During the past 30 years there has been a peaceful emancipatory progress in operation within the Republic of South Africa which is unprecedented in the world. The Transkei became independent without a shot being fired.*" 'Independence' was conferred on **Bophuthatswana**, and self-governing status on **KwaZulu** in 1977. **Venda** and **Ciskei** were also declared 'independent' in 1979 and 1981 respectively.

In this year the **first television broadcasts** were made in South Africa. Delays in the introduction of television, available in most parts of the world decades earlier, were due to government fears of the moral degeneration of the population, and of exposure to the 'pernicious' influence of international news and TV programming.

Political unrest in the townships and homelands reached crisis point by 1976. The township of Soweto, outside Johannesburg, where conditions were especially bleak, was the locus of the beginning of a massive national uprising.

THE SOWETO UPRISING

On 16 June 1976, pupils in Soweto staged a 15 000-strong protest march against the use of Afrikaans as a medium of instruction. Police opened fire on the protesters killing two. One of those killed was 12-year-old **Hector Pietersen**. A photograph of the fatally wounded child being carried away was published locally and in the world's press, bringing enormous international condemnation of the state's action.

In response to the police brutality, mobs rampaged through the streets of Soweto attacking the police and government buildings. Similar protests quickly spread across the country. Over the next year, nearly 600 people, including students, workers and activists, died in the course of protests, riots and militant confrontation with members of the security forces. Injuries numbered in the thousands. Arrests, deaths in detention and political trials followed the nation-wide revolt. Young militants had rocked the very foundations of the South African state, and had started a popular movement for freedom which would continue for the next two decades.

As a result of the student uprising, thousands of young black people left the country for exile. The uprising had introduced a note of urgency into the struggle for freedom in South Africa, though it was met with a massive crackdown on the part of the state. From this time, the idea of 'liberation before education' gained purchase among young activists. A generation of youth, sometimes referred to as 'the lost generation' sacrificed their education, taking on instead the mantle of the resistance struggle.

1977

In May 1977, **Winnie Mandela** (1934 –), then wife of Nelson Mandela, who had earlier been restricted to her home in Orlando, Soweto, was banished to the town of Brandfort in the Orange Free State. The order was served during a dawn raid and she and her family were immediately removed by police to Brandfort, where they were allocated a 3-roomed house without electricity or sanitation. During her eight-year banishment to Brandfort, Mandela became an important figure for many students and youth in the area.

STEVE BIKO (1942 – 1977)

In August of this year, Black Consciousness leader, Steve Biko, was detained by the police. During the 18 days of his detention, he was severely beaten and eventually taken, naked, handcuffed and manacled, in the back of a police vehicle from Port Elizabeth to Pretoria. On 12 September he died of severe head injuries in police custody. Minister of Police, Jimmy Kruger, was reported to have said that Biko's death 'left him cold'. His death prompted an international outcry. 15 000 people attended his burial in King William's Town in the eastern Cape.

In the same year the government placed **banning orders** on 17 anti-apartheid organisations. Among them were SASO, the Christian Institute and the BPC.

In this year **military conscription** for all white males was increased to two years.

Prime Minister Vorster said that discrimination would be eliminated in South Africa, but not in such a way as to create a multi-racial society. Dr Connie Mulder (Transvaal leader of the Nationalist Party) started referring to a '**plural democracy**' rather than separate development or apartheid.

During this time there was an increase in activity by security forces, particularly aimed at demolishing the informal settlements growing up around the cities where people flocked in an effort to get work. Churches in the Cape Town area became involved, and many parishes set up 'tent towns' on church property to house those whose shacks had been destroyed. The government had stopped building low-cost housing in an attempt to stem the urbanisation which was taking place, but this merely led to more crowded and squalid conditions.

1978

In January 1978 anti-apartheid activist and academic, **Rick Turner**, was killed by unidentified persons associated with the security forces in Durban. Frequently harassed by the police and under banning orders, Turner had been involved in trade union activities at the time of his death. In spite of inquests and investigations, including at the TRC, his killer has never been identified.

More and more anti-apartheid organisations came into being. In May 1978 the **Azanian Peoples' Organisation (AZAPO)** was launched. Within a Black Consciousness framework, AZAPO dedicated itself towards bringing about a common education and political system for all people. The following year saw the formation of the **Congress of South African Students (COSAS)**, **Port Elizabeth Black Civic Organisation (PEBCO)** and the **Azanian Students Organisation (AZASO)**, later renamed the **South African Students Congress (SASCO)**.

The destabilisation of neighbouring states was a clear objective of the Nationalist government. In 1978 the South African Defence Force (SADF) killed over 600 men, women and children at **Kassinga** in Angola. South African TV and radio denied activity by the SADF in Angola, although South African visitors overseas could see clear evidence of this incursion on television in other countries.

In 1978 Prime Minister B J Vorster was forced to resign in the wake of the **information scandal** which revealed that he agreed to channel millions of rands to the Department of Information for a major covert international propaganda campaign. The campaign included the launch of the Citizen newspaper in South Africa. **P W Botha** succeeded Vorster as Prime Minister. Botha brought to his administration the policy of 'total strategy' as a means of 'reforming' the apartheid system. What had been a state heavily dominated by the police under Vorster, now became a state extensively militarised under Botha.

1979

The relationship between **Inkatha** and the ANC deteriorated after a meeting in London between the leaderships of both parties. The two organisations failed to agree on the efficacy of protest politics, economic sanctions and the armed struggle as a means to bring an end to apartheid. Mangosuthu Buthelezi, who had become increasingly vocal on these matters, propounded instead investment and a free-market economy, and had mobilised a large Zulu constituency in his opposition to apartheid. The organisations' differing approaches to the struggle would later form the basis for the bitter and bloody political conflict which developed, particularly in Natal and later the Transvaal provinces, during the 80s.

Under Botha, the **State Security Council (SSC)** was established within the policy of 'total strategy'. The SSC came to function as an 'alternative' cabinet with its Secretariat at the centre of a total National Security Management System. Total Strategy was part of a programme of reform through which Botha would increase security measures in order to protect the country from the 'total onslaught' of Marxism. The implementation of the strategy was accompanied by several 'reforms' – described by many as 'too little, too late'.

The first of these reforms was the legalisation of **African trade unions** for the first time. In this Botha hoped to create the conditions for order in the labour movement and to prevent informal strike action which had so beleaguered big business and industry.

Botha also moved to dismantle aspects of **'petty' apartheid**, abolishing the Immorality and Mixed Marriages Acts, all segregation of amenities and the industrial colour bar. At the same time primary education was made compulsory and facilities for technical training were upgraded.

Previously some white private schools had been allowed to admit black students (African, coloured and Indian), according to a quota system.

1980
In 1980 Rhodesia gained its independence and became **Zimbabwe** after many years of a devastating civil war, international sanctions and world condemnation of the white administration of Prime Minister Ian Smith.

At the end of the 70s, Botha presented a programme of reform designed to undermine opposition by dealing with the country's security and economic problems. State security operations both at home and across the borders rose dramatically in the 80s. With umKhonto we Sizwe repositioning itself for a sustained guerrilla campaign and growing mobilisation of the trade union movement on a range of political issues, protests against the apartheid state were set to reach a pitch never seen before.

CHAPTER 9

THE TURBULENT EIGHTIES

1980 – 1989

From 1980 onwards, the move towards black majority rule seemed to be inevitable. It was a period characterised by ongoing public protests and the repressive and brutal response of the police to those engaged in resistance politics. Members of the SAP frequently resorted to firepower as a means of crowd control and clashes routinely broke out between police and protesters in public marches, demonstrations and at funerals. Funerals themselves were used as a forum for airing political grievances, especially when the deceased person/s had been activists or people killed by the security forces. It became commonplace to see security force vehicles, at times armoured tanks, flanking crowds at funerals and moving in to disperse mourners in an effort to curtail further mobilisation.

Members of the SAP also frequently used assault and torture as a means of extracting information from detainees, or to punish detainees for their alleged role in active community politics such as organised boycotts and protest actions. It is estimated that security forces kept files on 140 000 individuals and more than 9 000 organisations during this time.

With its back increasingly against the wall, the Nationalist government deployed emergency legislation and its security forces in heavy crackdowns on opposition both across the borders and at home where the struggle was now raging in the townships.

Nevertheless, progressive individuals within government understood that change must take place, and began to make courageous, though slow, moves towards bringing it about.

1980

School boycotts began in the Western Cape in April 1980 and spread to several other regions in South Africa. Grievances initially concerned the standard and quality of education, but these grew into wider political protest. Street protests and police actions resulted in widespread violence. In the Cape, police shootings led to over 40 deaths. In the Orange Free State police made use of force and fire power to break up crowd demonstrations, often resulting in injury and, in some cases, deaths. In Natal, boycotting pupils in KwaMashu defied Inkatha chief Buthelezi's calls to return to school, resulting in clashes between pupils and Inkatha supporters. These boycotts led to an increased exodus of youth from the country to join the ANC in exile.

1981

In January a raid by SADF troops on ANC targets in **Matola**, Mozambique, 20 people, including three SADF members, were killed. This was the first large-scale cross-border attack in the 1980s. Later in the year the SADF occupied a large part of Angola in 'Operation Protea'.

Several **high profile activists** were killed in this year. Student activist, Sizwe Kondile (1957 – 1981) of Port Elizabeth was abducted from Lesotho by the security police and killed; ANC chief representative in Zimbabwe, Joe Gqabi (1930 – 1981) was assassinated; Durban lawyer, Griffiths Mxenge, was also assassinated. Many such deaths were made to look like a purely criminal matter. However, former police captain Dirk Coetzee told a meeting of the Harms Commission in 1990 that the killings of Kondile and Mxenge had been police operations co-ordinated by himself.

In October 1980, Kobie Coetzee succeeded Jimmy Kruger as Minister of Justice. Coetzee began a programme of **prison reform**, allowing political prisoners access to newspapers and radio. Under Coetzee, several ANC members were transferred from Robben Island to Pollsmoor Prison, near Cape Town. These included Walter Sisulu, Ahmed Kathrada, Raymond Mhlaba and Andrew Mlangeni. Nelson Mandela was transferred to Pollsmoor in March of the following year. At around this time, a worldwide campaign for the release of South African political prisoners began under the banner of the 'Free Mandela Campaign'.

At the same time, Dr Piet Koornhof, Minister of Bantu Administration, stipulated that he would not allow Bantu and white typists to go on working in the same offices.

1982

Several more activists died at the hands of the security forces in this year. In February 1982, trade unionist, Neil Aggett (1954 – 1982), died in custody at **John Vorster Square**. Aggett had been detained for 70 days. Student activists, Siphiwe Mthimkulu (1963 – 1982) and Topsy Madaka (1954 – 1982) were abducted and killed by security police members. At the time of his death, Mthimkulu had initiated legal proceedings against the police for poisoning him with thallium while he was in detention. ANC chief representative in Swaziland, Petrus 'Nzima' Nyawose (1945 – 1982) and his wife were killed in a car bomb explosion while Ruth First (1925 – 1982), an activist academic at the university in Maputo, was killed by a parcel bomb despatched by the security police.

In 1982, right wingers in the National Party feared more reform under the leadership of P W Botha. F W de Klerk (1936 –) took over leadership of the Nationalist Party in the Transvaal, and Andries Treurnicht (d.1993) broke away to form the new **Conservative Party (CP)**.

Also in this year the **ANC London offices** were bombed by a South African security police team headed by senior Military Intelligence operative, Craig Williamson.

The year ended in another large-scale **cross-border raid** conducted by the SADF. On 9 December South African commandos were airlifted into Maseru, Lesotho, where they went on a shooting rampage in search of ANC refugees and operatives. Forty-two people were killed, 12 of them Lesotho nationals.

1983

MK stepped up its guerrilla campaign in urban areas inside the country. In a systematic **bombing campaign**, security force personnel and military installations were targeted. Increasingly, civilians fell victim to the blasts.

THE PRETORIA BOMB

On 29 May 1983, MK members detonated an explosive device outside the administrative headquarters of the South African Air Force (SAAF) in Church Street, Pretoria. Twenty-one people were killed and 219 injured in this attack. Eleven of the dead and up to 84 of the injured were SAAF employees. Two others killed were the MK operatives who had executed the attack. The remaining casualties and injuries were civilians.

In retaliation, the following week, security forces launched a retaliatory raid on a suburb in Maputo, Mozambique, killing six people, including a child in a crèche.

1983

In 1983 a new constitution was adopted by parliament. The new constitution provided for the creation of a '**tricameral parliament**' consisting of three legislative houses for whites, coloureds and Indians accountable to the President's Council. A national whites-only referendum the following year endorsed the tricameral project. For most blacks, coloureds and Indians, the idea was nonsense and was widely boycotted.

When the new constitution came into force it was met with **protests and riots** throughout South Africa. In response to these protests, which hinged on a range of issues, including proposed rent hikes, the state began to use SADF troops to do the work of policing the townships. In 1984, 7 000 troops were moved into the township of Sebokeng to quell rioting. Minister of Law and Order, Louis le Grange, described the situation as: "It is war, plain and simple". In some parts of the country a State of Emergency was declared.

The **United Democratic Front (UDF)** was launched in Mitchell's Plain, Cape Town, on 20 August, primarily in opposition to the introduction of the tricameral parliament and black municipal councils. As an umbrella body, the UDF grew rapidly in size, attracting hundreds of affiliates in a broad range of anti-apartheid organisations. The UDF shared with the ANC a fundamental determination to bring about a non-racial and unitary democracy in South Africa, and while some of its affiliate organisations took care to maintain their political neutrality, it was increasingly identified with the ANC. It was able to mobilise masses of people under its banner and was at the forefront of the wave of pro-democracy demonstrations over the next eight years. It was dissolved in August 1991 after the unbanning of the ANC and during the transition to democracy.

One of those to affiliate was the **End Conscription Campaign (ECC)** which was launched to formalise opposition to military conscription.

STATE OF EMERGENCY

A State of Emergency was declared on 20 July 1985 in terms of Section 2(1) of the Public Safety Act of 1953. It affected 36 magisterial districts in the Cape, Transvaal and the Orange Free State, and was extended to eight other areas on 26 October. It was lifted on 7 March 1986 and re-imposed again on 12 June 1986, this time affecting the whole of the country. The State of Emergency was re-imposed in June every year until the April 1994 elections.

From the mid-80s thousands of people were detained under Emergency regulations which gave the police power to detain persons on the merest suspicion that they were a 'threat' to state security. With a clampdown on the media's reporting of the 'unrest', it often became difficult for families to find information about a person's detention. Many hundreds of detainees emerged from custody with accounts of assault, torture, solitary confinement and lack of access to proper legal representation or medical care. The Detainees' Parents' Support Committee and the Education Crisis Committee were set up to monitor the implementation of Emergency rule and to offer support to detainees' families.

Clamps on **media freedom** were felt heavily in this period. Restrictions on the press and other progressive publications placed huge challenges before the media community. Not allowed to publish articles on unrest or repression, some had to resort to printing with blacked out words, phrases or sentences to ensure that readers were aware of the censorship.

1984

Bishop Desmond Tutu (1931 –) was awarded the Nobel Peace Prize in recognition for his contribution towards challenging the government to move to democratic change.

In this year South Africa and Angola signed the **Lusaka agreement** securing South Africa's withdrawal from Angola. In reality South Africa failed to withdraw completely. At around the same time South Africa and Mozambique signed the **Nkomati Accord** which committed both sides to cease hostile actions against each other. In the accord Mozambique also agreed to expel ANC military personnel from Mozambican territory.

At home **demonstrations and protests** increased steadily. Troop activity in the townships, rent boycotts and consumer boycotts were rallying points of these protests. In Sharpeville protests at a rent increase resulted in the deaths of nine people. With a UDF-backed campaign to render the townships 'ungovernable' and expose the illegitimacy of the regime, pressures were heaped on the government to hasten the progress of reform. From outside the country, these pressures took the form of trade sanctions and a cultural and sporting boycott.

Many people within South Africa, including Inkatha leader **Mangosuthu Buthelezi**, did not support sanctions as they felt that they would hurt the poor. Bishop Tutu supported sanctions to force change, but was very unpopular with some of his conservative church members for his stance.

1985

P W Botha, now State President, offered to release **Nelson Mandela** and other political prisoners only if they unconditionally rejected violence as a tool to attain their political ends. Mandela refused to be released with any preconditions. At a rally in Soweto to honour Bishop Tutu's Nobel Peace Prize, Mandela's daughter, Zinzi, spoke on behalf of her father saying he was not prepared to accept his freedom at the expense of the freedom of the organisation, and that: "Only free men can negotiate."

On 21 March 1985, members of the SAP in **Langa**, Uitenhage, Cape, opened fire on mourners marching to the prohibited funeral of four youths killed by the police. At least 20 people were killed in this incident and many others were injured. Police had been issued with heavy ammunition following a decision to take stronger measures to restore public order. This was the order of the day as the police resorted to fire power to quell 'disturbances' and protests in towns and cities across the country.

The political situation was by now spiralling out of control. Under renewed declarations of a State of Emergency, the police had appeared to lose control completely as a climate of **lawlessness** developed in townships across the country. Instead informal or 'kangaroo' courts were coming into being in which UDF-supporting activists, referred to as 'comrades', began punishing alleged 'traitors' or collaborators with necklacing, which involved using a car tyre filled with petrol to burn victims, frequently to death. Police recorded 406 such 'necklace' killings and 395 deaths by burning between September 1984 and December 1989, a third of these taking place in the Eastern Cape and Border regions. The practice was condoned by Winnie Mandela who said in a speech at the time:

"Together, hand-in-hand with our sticks and matches, with our necklaces, we shall liberate this country".

UDF supporters in urban and rural areas across the country frequently carried out attacks on symbols of authority, including police and community councillors.

Vigilante groups (sponsored clandestinely by the security forces) and members of the security forces themselves carried out counter attacks on UDF activists.

THE TROJAN HORSE

Police carried out several 'Trojan horse'-style attacks on activists. In Despatch (eastern Cape) on 18 April 1985, a municipal truck loaded with branches drove past the Nomathamsanqa Higher Primary School. Scholars were on boycott at the time but were playing games in the school grounds. The truck was stopped by youth in the street. The driver got out and fired a shot into the air, at which police officers emerged from under the branches and opened fire on the group of youths, hitting six people. Four died and two survived. Again, on 2 May at Uitenhage (eastern Cape), police members, concealed under a load of cardboard boxes on a municipal truck, opened fire on people gathered at the scene of an accident involving a Hippo (armoured vehicle) in Mabandla Road, KwaNobuhle. One person was killed. In October 1985, members of the South African Railway Police, hiding in wooden crates on the back of a railway truck opened fire on a crowd of protesters in Athlone, Cape Town, killing three youths and injuring several others. The operation was repeated in Crossroads the following day, killing a further two youths.

1985

Four members of the **Port Elizabeth Black Civic Organisation** (**PEBCO**), an affiliate of the UDF, were abducted on 8 May 1985 by members of the Port Elizabeth Security Branch, taken to Post Chalmers and killed. Their bodies were subsequently thrown into the Fish River.

THE CRADOCK FOUR

Four eastern Cape UDF activists were abducted and assassinated by members of the security police on 27 June 1985 as they drove back to Cradock from a meeting in Port Elizabeth. The four were Matthew Goniwe, Sparrow Mkhonto and Fort Calata from Cradock, and Sicelo Mhlauli from Oudtshoorn. Before their deaths, all had been frequently detained, tortured and harassed by the police. Their deaths sparked a national outcry and resulted in street protests in many regions across the country.

1985

On 26 June, eight young activists were killed and at least seven were injured in explosions involving booby-trapped hand grenades in Duduza, KwaThema and Tsakane, Transvaal. The zero-timed grenades had been provided by a Vlakplaas operative purporting to be an MK operative. The operation, codenamed **'Zero Zero'**, had been authorised by the Minister of Law and Order.

While losing the war on the home front, the state continued to engage across its borders. On 14 June 1985, SADF Special Forces, together with members of the Security branch, launched a cross-border attack on ANC targets in **Gaborone**, Botswana. Twelve people were killed and six were wounded in the operation. Among those killed were eight South Africans, two Botswana nationals, a Lesotho and a Somali citizen. The ANC claimed that only five of those killed had links with the organisation. Later in the year, security forces launched another raid on **Maseru**, killing six South Africans including MK operatives.

THE DEATH OF VICTORIA MXENGE

Victoria Mxenge, a Durban attorney and wife of slain Griffiths Mxenge, was assassinated in Umlazi on 1 August, triggering a rapid escalation of conflict in Natal, principally between the UDF and Inkatha. At a memorial service for Mrs Mxenge in the Umlazi cinema on 8 August 1985, 17 people were killed and 20 injured when members of the amaButho, an Inkatha-based 'community guard force', launched an attack on the mourners.

Mrs Mxenge was buried in East London two days later. After her funeral in Duncan Village, returning mourners carried out arson attacks on various buildings including the rent office, schools, a beer hall, a bottle store, a community centre and the homes of six community councillors, police officers and suspected collaborators. Violence continued on the following days with looting and burning of commercial and delivery vehicles, and running battles between youths and members of the security forces. Five people were dead by 14 August. By 16 August, the toll had risen to 19 people dead and 138 injured.

1985

On 28 August, thousands of marchers set off from different points in Cape Town to **Pollsmoor prison** to demand the release of Nelson Mandela. The marches were violently disrupted by police. Nine people were killed that day and by the end of the week the death toll had risen to 28. The event sparked the outbreak of street protests and severe unrest across Cape Town until the end of the year.

The **Congress of South African Trade Unions (COSATU)** was launched in November. It quickly positioned itself at the forefront of the rising tide of opposition to the apartheid government.

1985

In December of this year five people were killed and over 60 injured in an explosion at a shopping centre in **Amanzimtoti**, near Durban. MK operative, Sibusiso Andrew Zondo (1967 – 1986), was convicted for the bombing and executed in September 1986. Zondo told the trial court that his actions had been precipitated by the December 1985 SADF raid on Maseru and his feeling that violence was: *"the only option for changing the lives of black people in South Africa"*.

Towards the end of 1985, the UDF adopted a campaign to make the **townships ungovernable**. Educational institutions and trade unions became sites of revolutionary struggle. School boycotts and strikes transformed into scenes of violent conflict and bloodletting. A State of Emergency was declared in July and extended in October.

UDF-Inkatha conflict in Natal spread rapidly. Deaths from these conflicts amounted to over 15 000 during the next decade. By 1990 there were almost 1 million residents of KwaZulu-Natal[1] who were living in 'internal exile', displaced from their homes and communities. The conflict soon spread to townships on the Rand. Hundreds of thousands of people had their houses burned to the ground, and all their possessions destroyed.

[1] From around this time KwaZulu and Natal territories were distinct from one another. During the period of transition in the early 1990s and as the KwaZulu Administration was dismantled, all areas in the province came to be known as KwaZulu/Natal and, following the April 1994 elections, as KwaZulu-Natal.

P W Botha delivered his famous '**Crossing the Rubicon**' speech at the National Party's annual congress in Durban. Raising hopes for a real programme of political reform, he said: "*I believe that we are today crossing the Rubicon in South Africa. There is no turning back*". However, there was no real evidence of reform to support the statement. Indeed, he said: "*I am not prepared to lead white South Africans and other minority groups on a road to abdication and suicide*".

1985

Trouble simmered in the **homelands** during this period. In the Transkei, Prime Minister George Matanzima was ousted by the Transkei Defence Force in September 1985, and Stella Sigcau was installed. She herself was deposed three months later in a coup under Bantu Holomisa.

In the homeland territory of QwaQwa, mass protests broke out in response to a presidential proclamation incorporating Botshabelo into the homeland. Conflict broke out between UDF and Inkatha supporters in Natal over the proposed incorporation of Clermont, outside Durban, into KwaZulu territory.

1986

From 1985 various interest groups (including church groups, trade unions, 'Afrikaners', business groups) met with the **ANC in exile** to discuss the growing crisis in South Africa and to formulate a vision for a 'post-apartheid' South Africa.

The attorney **George Bizos** visited Oliver Tambo in Lusaka. He gave him news of Mandela's medical condition, and assured the ANC that Mandela was not acting on his own, and that he would consult the party leadership before any important decisions were made.

THE GUGULETU SEVEN

On 3 March 1986, seven men aged between 16 and 23 were shot dead in a field at Guguletu, Cape Town. Police claimed that the victims were known 'terrorists' and had been killed during a legitimate anti-terrorist operation. A magistrate at two inquests made the same finding. Later it was revealed that the security forces had created an elaborate cover-up of their involvement in the incident. Security Branch members from Cape Town and Vlakplaas infiltrated askaris (co-opted former freedom fighters, working as black undercover policemen) into a group of seven activists, planned an ambush of police personnel to lure the youths into a trap, then killed them. This was not the only incident involving the security force's use of ambush and entrapment to lure activists and MK operatives to their deaths during this period.

1986

During this year Malcolm Frazer (Australian Prime Minister) and Olusegun Obsanjo (former military ruler of Nigeria) visited South Africa as part of an **Eminent Persons' Group**. They managed to meet with Mr Mandela on several occasions for discussions.

On 19 May, during the visit of the Eminent Persons' Group, the SADF attacked the neighbouring states of Zambia, Zimbabwe and Botswana. The group was horrified and left the country, recommending economic sanctions against South Africa be maintained and increased.

Mr Mandela asked to see President P W Botha in an attempt to defuse the situation of neighbouring states being attacked. Mr Coetzee (Minister of Justice) acted as an intermediary.

The head of the Broederbond met with Thabo Mbeki (1942 –) and Oliver Tambo in New York for **talks** about the **transition**. De Lange maintained that, in spite of Afrikaners wanting to maintain their cultural identity, he needed to persuade the government to move away from apartheid.

With the withdrawal of foreign investment and the leverage of **sanctions**, the country's economy was in a state of crisis. The government held out against both internal and international pressure to bring an end to apartheid. Instead, Botha chose to renew the State of Emergency in July 1986, this time encompassing the whole country. 'Security' spending increased with more and more funds being channelled into the work of clandestine state forces and vigilante movements. Many pro-democracy activists fell victim to a shadowy and loose network of state-sponsored 'hit squads'. The political violence besetting the country at the time was described by the state as 'black-on-black'.

In 1986 the SADF ran a **paramilitary training for Inkatha recruits** in the Caprivi Strip. Clandestine negotiations between Inkatha and the government over the previous year had resulted in the state's agreeing to help provide Inkatha with a covert military capacity. The trainees were later deployed in areas around KwaZulu-Natal, against the political enemies of the state and Inkatha, namely the UDF and ANC, and their allies.

On 14 June 1986, MK operatives detonated a car bomb outside the Parade Hotel on the Durban beachfront. The explosion killed three women and injured at least 74 other people in the *Why Not Bar* and adjacent **Magoo's Bar**. MK operative Robert McBride was sentenced to death for the bombing. His sentence was later commuted to life imprisonment. He was released from prison in 1992 in an agreement forged during the process of negotiations.

THE MANDELA UNITED FOOTBALL CLUB (MUFC)

The MUFC was established in late 1986 when Winnie Mandela (married to Nelson Mandela between 1958 and 1992) was instrumental in resolving an internal conflict in the Soweto Youth Congress. Youths involved in the conflict set up the football club and moved into the outbuildings of the Mandela home in Orlando West, Soweto, Johannesburg, and – after this was burnt down – at her home in Diepkloof extension. In 1987, the first allegations of brutality were levelled against the youths. Later their behaviour was described by community residents as a 'reign of terror'. Club members, and Winnie Mandela herself, were implicated directly or indirectly in a range of incidents, including assaults and abduction, and the murder and attempted murder of several individuals. In September 1990, Winnie Mandela and seven others were charged with kidnapping and assault in the events leading to the 1988 death of the young activist, Stompie Moeketsi. In 1991 Winnie Mandela was found guilty of the charges and received a six-year prison sentence. She was released on bail pending an appeal. In the same year Winnie Mandela, who enjoyed massive grassroots support, was elected to the ANC's National Executive Committee and as President of the ANC Women's League. She held this position until May 1992, when the entire executive was suspended, and was re-elected as president in December 1993.

1987

In the '**Midlands War**' in Natal, conflict and violence continued between supporters and Inkatha and the UDF as each attempted to carve inroads into opposing territory. The conflict raged on for three years and was exacerbated by the deployment of Inkatha-aligned 'special constables'.

KITSKONSTABELS

Known colloquially as 'kitskonstabels' (instant police), Special Constables were recruited from urban and rural areas, and were usually unemployed African men with few educational qualifications. Many were illiterate and some had criminal convictions. Training was conducted in September 1986 at the SAP's Koeberg facility outside Cape Town and consisted of a six-week course, later increased to three months. The training was perfunctory and involved only one seven-hour course in riot drill. In the training the UDF and ANC were presented as the enemy to be suppressed.

By the end of the 1980s, approximately 8 000 special constables had been recruited, trained and deployed in urban and rural towns across the country where unrest was the strongest. In Natal (later known as KwaZulu-Natal), they were used to bolster **Inkatha** in areas around Pietermaritzburg and the Natal Midlands. They rapidly became associated with numerous violations both on and off duty, and were the subject of several interdicts. Special constables were themselves victims of attacks by both civilian opposition groups and the armed forces of the liberation movements.

1987

High profile ANC activists continued to be targeted for **assassination** by covert units in the security forces. In April 1987 lawyer Albie Sachs was severely injured in a car bomb explosion in Maputo. Also in April, ANC activist, Gibson Mondlane, died after drinking poisoned beer brought into Maputo from South Africa by a security police operative. Later in the year Joan and Jeremy Brickhill were injured in a car bomb explosion in Harare.

1987

In the general elections in May, the **Conservative Party** replaced the Progressive Federal Party as the official opposition in parliament.

In an initiative led by political academic, Frederick van Zyl Slabbert and poet, Breyten Breytenbach, a group of white, mostly Afrikaans-speaking academics and politically influential figures travelled to Dakar, Senegal, for talks with the leadership of the ANC-in-exile. The historic meeting debated intensively the crisis of apartheid rule, the spiral of violence at home, and the strategy and perspectives of the ANC. It agreed unanimously that a negotiated settlement was the only way forward in South Africa. Dubbed the **Dakar safari**, the meeting with the ANC was reviled by some and applauded by others. Several similar safaris by other groups followed, leading to a growing consciousness at home that the ANC would be part of a political solution. It was the beginning of a concerted process of reconciliation in South Africa.

1987

In November, **Govan Mbeki** (father of State President Thabo Mbeki) was released after negotiations between Mandela, Coetzee and others. Upon release he was placed under restriction orders.

Operation Vula (from the word 'Vulindlela' – open the road) was launched by the ANC with the aim of infiltrating MK operatives into the country to build structures in preparation for the return of ANC leaders to South Africa.

1988

In yet further unrest in the homelands, an attempted coup in **Bophuthatswana**, from within the ranks of the Bophuthatswana Defence Force, was crushed by the SADF in February.

In February, 18 organisations including the UDF and Cosatu were placed under severe **restriction orders**.

The year saw more **state sponsored attacks** on individual activists, both at home and abroad. Some activists died in police custody.

STANZA BOPAPE (1961 – 1988)

In June 1988, a Pretoria activist, Stanza Bopape, died in detention after having been tortured. Police claimed that he had escaped and 'disappeared'. His body was allegedly thrown into the crocodile-infested Komati River at Komatipoort. Several members of the security forces applied to the Truth and Reconciliation Commission for amnesty both for Bopape's killing and for the deliberate attempt to cover up the truth. One of the applicants, Major A P van Niekerk, described to the Commission the circumstances in which Bopape was killed. He said:

"We decided to tie Mr Bopape to a chair ... His shirt was removed, his hands were tied to the supports of the chair and his feet to the legs ... Sergeant du Preez had the shock device in his hand ... There were two cords running from the device and at the tip of these cords, there were two pieces of cloth which were wrapped around the tips of the cords. This device was turned three or four times by Sergeant du Preez and whilst he was turning it, Mr Engelbrecht pushed these cords against his body ... It didn't take very long, maybe two to four minutes, the device was turned, then it was stopped, then someone asked him if he wanted to say something and if there was no reaction to that, then the machine was turned again and this must have happened about three times. By the third time, Mr Bopape's head fell forward and I realised there was something wrong. We immediately untied him, placed him on the floor and Sergeant du Preez gave him mouth-to-mouth resuscitation. It seemed that he was dead already and I think that all of us standing there ... all thought that he was dead".

1988

Members of the security forces also carried out covert operations on buildings associated with the UDF and underground ANC. In September, **Khotso House**, the headquarters of the South African Council of Churches (SACC) in Johannesburg, was bombed. Eight years later a former police commissioner

told the Truth Commission that he ordered the attack and that the order had emanated from as high as the presidency itself.

The following month, the offices of the **South African Catholic Bishops' Conference (SACBC)** at Khanya House was destroyed in an arson attack.

Right-wing attacks on people were becoming more frequent. In November **Barend Strydom**, who claimed membership of several right-wing organisations, opened fire indiscriminately at black people in Strijdom Square, Pretoria, killing six people and injuring sixteen.

In 1988, 166 cases of **AIDS (Acquired Immune Deficiency Syndrome)** were reported in South Africa. By the late 1990s, up to a third of the population of some regions was said to be HIV positive or infected with full blown AIDS.

THE TRUST FEEDS MASSACRE

An attack on supposed UDF supporters was planned by riot, security and local policemen and Inkatha members in the Trust Feeds area of the Natal Midlands in December 1988. It began when members of the SAP and the Riot Unit arrested known UDF supporters at Trust Feeds, New Hanover, near Pietermaritzburg, on 2 December 1988 and withdrew their presence from the area, leaving UDF-supporting families particularly vulnerable to attack. The next day, 3 December 1988, four special constables stormed in and opened fire on an all-night prayer vigil in a house believed by the perpetrators to be occupied by UDF supporters. Eleven people were killed. None of the victims or survivors were UDF supporters. An SAP member and four Special Constables were convicted for the murders. In their defence they alleged that senior Inkatha leaders were part of the planning.

As the 80s drew to a close various initiatives were taken to foster talks between South African groups, including the government, and the ANC in exile. One of these exchanges involved the State President's brother, Wimpie de Klerk. The outcome of these informal talks was a fundamental change in attitude in parts of the Afrikaner community. A special group of government negotiators was formed. To make Nelson Mandela more accessible for talks, he was moved from Pollsmoor Prison to Victor Verster Prison near

Franschhoek. He was given a house in which to live and a personal warder to attend to his needs.

1989

At the beginning of the year, activists held in detention embarked on a **hunger strike** to pressurise the authorities into releasing them. Some of the detainees had spent over three years in detention without trial.

In April 1989, the **Democratic Party**, amalgamating three white political parties left of the National Party, was launched.

In May 1989, academic **David Webster** was shot and killed in a suburban Johannesburg street by members of the CCB.

CIVIL CO-OPERATION BUREAU (CCB)

Secret operations of the security forces led to the setting up of the Civil Co-operation Bureau (CCB) in the mid- to late 80s. The CCB endeavoured to pre-empt resistance operations by setting up a complex network of 'civilian' businesses and business fronts, run by trained and trusted security forces personnel, to channel operational intelligence to the bureau.

The CCB, which frequently convened at Vlakplaas (a clandestine security force farm base outside Pretoria), was hardly responsible for the promotion of civilian co-operation. Instead it planned and executed covert operations directed against individual activists and activist groups both at home and abroad.

Other campaigns included disinformation campaigns to discredit high-profile anti-apartheid figures and the incrimination of the 'enemy' through the sabotage of state targets. In planning operations, CCB members had access to specialised weapons produced by a covert SADF division, and toxic substances supplied by the covert Chemical and Biological Warfare programme.

Victims of CCB operations ranged from high-profile opponents of the regime, such as the September 1989 killing of Anton Lubowski, Secretary-General of SWAPO in Windhoek, and the March 1988 killing of ANC Chief Representative in Paris, Dulcie September to others who were less well-known and disappeared without trace.

In July 1989, the ANC, Cosatu and the UDF adopted the **Harare Declaration**, a policy document laying down conditions for moving towards a negotiated political settlement. The pre-conditions included lifting the State of Emergency, legalising political organisations, releasing political prisoners, lifting restrictions on political activity and suspending political executions. In return the ANC would suspend the armed struggle.

At home a mass **defiance campaign** was launched by the Mass Democratic Movement (MDM) which had grown out of the heavily restricted UDF. The MDM was a loose coalition of hundreds of pro-democracy groups both inside and outside the UDF and was perhaps the largest anti-apartheid lobby ever to take to the streets. A group of black men who tried to catch a bus reserved for whites in Pretoria were arrested and threatened with charges of 'conspiracy'. They were part of the peaceful defiance campaign against segregation of bus services.

1989

State President **P W Botha** had a stroke. Nelson Mandela wrote to him, pointing out that majority rule did not mean black domination, and asking for talks between the government and the ANC to create a proper climate for negotiations, and to move towards a new dispensation. Botha said he was ready to talk. A meeting was arranged at Tuynhuis in the Gardens, Cape Town. It was held at night so that nobody would recognise Mandela and know that the meeting was taking place.

Encounters between the ANC in exile and various interest groups at home continued and increased dramatically at this time. Up to 150 white South Africans, representatives of 35 opposition organisations, met with the ANC in Lusaka and Zimbabwe.

1989

By 1989 the **Soviet Union** was disintegrating and the Berlin Wall was brought down the following year. The extent and nature of the communist 'threat' had to be reappraised world-wide. In South Africa F W de Klerk used the opportunity to liberalise government strategy. He was however quoted in the

Weekly Mail[1] saying: *"The government has no intention of putting each race into a separate compartment. However, we would never accept integration"*. A year later he was quoted as saying: *"I have been in Parliament for 17 years, and I have never defended the concept of apartheid"*.

1989

In September **F W de Klerk** took over from P W Botha as president. There was a general election, and de Klerk admitted saying that: *"the country is now irrevocably on the road of drastic change"*. He drew his cabinet together to discuss policy formulation and negotiations to move towards black, majority rule. On three occasions he met with Mandela at Tuynhuis where they discussed the transition to democracy. In spite of the start of serious talks about democratisation, some were still very resistant. Director of Information, Dr Con Botha is quoted as saying: *"We are not going soft on the ANC. In fact, the ball is on the other foot"*. Leon Wessels was the first Nationalist minister to make a public apology for apartheid, and it became obvious that change was about to come.

Walter Sisulu and five other ANC life prisoners were released and were welcomed at a mass rally in Soweto. For the first time in many years the flags of banned liberation movements were seen fluttering against the Johannesburg skyline. It was only a matter of time before the ban would be lifted.

[1] 8 August 1989

CHAPTER 10

TRANSITION TO DEMOCRACY

1990 – 1994

The early 1990s saw the beginning of an unprecedented wave of political changes in South Africa. In the face of ongoing international sanctions, the country's economy had declined seriously and showed little sign of recovery. Unemployment and inflation simply had to be addressed in ways which were not permissible with apartheid legislation. Moreover with growing international condemnation of apartheid and a wholly uncontainable groundswell of protests at home, the government had its back against the wall.

With the collapse of Soviet communism and the dismantling of the Berlin Wall, the 'red threat' no longer seemed to cloud the horizon for white South Africa. It was an era which saw a palpable rise in the 'global village'. With rapid developments in technology, nations could no longer hold out in isolation. Electronic communications and the World Wide Web were about to dramatically transform the way individuals and groups transacted from their place in local, national and global networks.

1990

On 2 February, F W de Klerk opened parliament by announcing **sweeping changes** in the political landscape of the country. The ANC, PAC, SACP and other organisations were unbanned, media restrictions were lifted, the death penalty was suspended pending further review, and several high profile prisoners, including Nelson Mandela, were to be unconditionally released.

The announcement was greeted with euphoria by most South Africans and with anger by right-wing organisations who began to mobilise their members for a white 'counter-revolution'.

It was evident that real change was about to occur. South Africa was the most powerful country in Africa, with a gross domestic product of $104 billion – making up 60% of that of the entire sub-Saharan Africa.

Change would only come, however, at a high price.

On 11 February **Nelson Mandela** was released after 27 years in jail. At a 100 000-strong rally in Durban two weeks later, Mandela urged people to throw their pangas (machetes) and guns 'into the sea' and to end the violence in KwaZulu-Natal which had claimed more than 2 500 lives in the previous five years.

1990

In March representatives of the government met with an ANC delegation, headed by Mandela, to discuss conditions for a process of negotiations.

March also saw upheaval in the homelands with the **Ciskei** administration of Lennox Sebe (1926 – 1994) falling in a military coup led by Brigadier Oupa Gqozo (1952 –) who established an interim administration pending the introduction of a full democracy in the country. The following month, the homeland government in **Venda** also fell in a coup led by Gabriel Ramushwana. He too announced an interim administration until such time as the territory would be incorporated in a unitary South Africa.

On 26 March, 14 people were killed and hundreds were injured in **Sebokeng**, near Johannesburg when police opened fire on protesters at a rally to oppose high rents and segregated facilities such as schools. A commission of enquiry into the shootings headed by Justice Richard Goldstone found the police had used excessive force in crowd control. Following the shootings, ANC leaders called off talks with the government.

Also in March, **Namibia** became an independent country. Nelson Mandela was given a rapturous welcome when he attended the presidential inauguration of Mr Sam Nujoma of the South West Africa People's Organisation (SWAPO).

In April, members of a far-right group broke into an arsenal at Air Force headquarters in Pretoria and stole artillery in preparation for a campaign to resist the tide of change rushing towards democratic rule in the country.

In April, four years exactly before the date of the first democratic election, **ANC leaders**, Thabo Mbeki, Joe Slovo (1926 – 1995) and others returned to the country from exile. Mbeki later became President of the second ANC-led government while Slovo, also a leader of the South African Communist Party, would play a key role in negotiating the new constitution.

In May 1990 talks between the Nationalist government and the ANC were resumed. In what became known as the **Groote Schuur minute**, agreement was reached on the conditions necessary for negotiations. These included the release of political prisoners and the repatriation of political exiles, and the gradual lifting of the nationwide State of Emergency towards bringing an end to political violence in the country. Later in August the ANC and the government issued a joint declaration (the **Pretoria minute**) committing both sides to working towards reducing levels of political violence in the country. The government would work hard to end the State of Emergency in Natal (later known as KwaZulu-Natal). The ANC would move towards suspending the armed struggle.

Violent **political conflict** between Inkatha and ANC supporters in Natal (later known as KwaZulu-Natal) and in townships to the south-east of Johannesburg had reached critical proportions. During August, more than 500 people died in 11 days of fighting between residents of townships in the PWV region and hostel-dwellers, largely migrant Zulu workers. In response, the government re-imposed a State of Emergency in the region. In many instances police were accused of assisting Inkatha supporters to carry out attacks on UDF and ANC supporters. Defence Force troops were deployed in townships when police were accused of making insufficient efforts to curb the violence.

TRAIN VIOLENCE

Train commuters on the East Rand became the victims of violent attacks by unknown forces, frequently including opportunistic criminal elements. The Truth Commission would later hear evidence that members of the security forces, or a 'third force', were at work to fan the flames of enmity between ANC and Inkatha supporters, contributing to the general destabilisation of South African society during the process of negotiations. Sometimes the perpetrators were identified as Inkatha supporters when they were seen coming from Inkatha-dominated hostels, or when they wore red headbands and chanted 'Usuthu', a war-cry associated with the Zulu-dominated Inkatha. These allegations were confirmed in the findings of the Goldstone Commission of Enquiry into train violence in the southern Transvaal, which heard evidence that train attacks were in fact planned in and executed from hostels in the area.

WHITE RIGHT-WING BACKLASH

Believing F W de Klerk's reform initiatives to be traitorous to the Afrikaner cause, in the early 1990s white right-wing organisations instituted an orchestrated campaign of mass demonstration and sabotage to protest against the unfolding democratic process in the country. Perhaps the two most dramatic of these mass actions were firstly, the occupation in June 1993 by members of the AWB and other right-wing groups of the World Trade Centre at Kempton Park, where constitutional negotiations were underway, and secondly, the invasion by members of the AWB of Bophut-hatswana in support of the homeland administration in 1994.

In early 1990 right-wing organisations including the Witwolwe (white wolves) carried out a bombing campaign, targeting blacks, Jews and 'liberal' white politicians. On 6 July, 27 people were injured when the Witwolwe detonated a powerful bomb at a bus and taxi terminus in Johannesburg. At the end of November 1990 the Afrikaner Weerstandsbeweging (AWB) adopted the so-called 'white-by-night' policy in terms of which black people were denied the right to be in so-called white areas after 21h00. AWB members set up road blocks and tried to enforce a white-by-night curfew in small towns where they were most organised.

Photographers and journalists were thrown out of AWB meetings, some severely injured in beatings and attacks.

Schools were targeted for sabotage attacks. Following announcements that the Group Areas Act was to be repealed and schools would be opened to all races, a number of schools were destroyed in a series of bomb blasts.

1990

In July 1990 the **Inkatha** cultural movement reconstituted itself as a political party under the leadership of Mangosuthu Buthelezi. The **South African Communist Party (SACP)** was also re-established at a 40 000-strong rally in Soweto. The SACP was formally launched in Durban a year later under the leadership of Joe Slovo. Eighteen months later Chris Hani replaced Slovo as General Secretary.

Later in July over 40 members of the ANC and SACP, including senior member 'Mac' Maharaj were detained for allegedly attempting to overthrow the government through operation Vula.

From October 1990, processes were set in motion for the **repeal** of various discriminatory pieces of legislation. At the same time the formerly whites-only National Party agreed to accept South Africans of all races as members of the party. With the systematic repeal of apartheid legislation over the next few years, various countries announced an end to their cultural and sporting boycotts on South Africa. A year later a South African cricket team travelled to Calcutta where it played three one-day international matches against India.

Also in October, **Nic Cruise** was killed when he opened a parcel bomb delivered to a computer company in Durban. The company serviced various trade unions and anti-apartheid organisations and several of its employees were ANC members. The police detained six right-wingers in connection with a range of incidents including the killing of Cruise.

In November, at a widely representative meeting of the **churches** in Rustenburg, the Dutch Reformed Church made a 'confession of sin' for its role in propping up the apartheid system over years. Many churches had previously described apartheid as a 'heresy' and a 'crime against humanity'.

In December, ANC President **Oliver Tambo** returned to the country after 30 years in exile in time for the ANC's first conference on South African soil in 31 years. The conference pronounced 1991 to be the 'year of mass action'. It also approved the creation of 'self-defence units' to protect grassroots communities from attack in the widespread political violence taking place in the country.

1991

When F W de Klerk opened parliament in February 1991, he announced that legislation would be introduced to repeal of the Land Acts, the Group Areas Act, the Development of Black Communities Act and most significantly, the Population Registration Act. This meant that **racial classification was a thing of the past** and that, in principle, people could no longer be discriminated against by virtue of their racial or ethnic identities. At this time black children were admitted to 205 white government schools across the country for the first time. Most white government schools, however, voted against this move.

The first group of **political exiles** returned and 40 **political prisoners** were released under the terms of the Pretoria Minute in March 1991. At the same time indemnity from prosecution was granted to over 2 500 MK members, anti-apartheid activists and members of some right-wing groups.

Many political exiles found themselves in difficult positions. It was hard to get work on their return, and their families had huge expectations of their ability to provide, having been trained in other countries. This was very challenging and many returnees found it difficult to re-integrate into their families, communities and society.

In 1991 leaders of the **ANC** and the **IFP** met on several occasions in an attempt to end violence between their supporters on the ground. Violence continued unabated however with 22 people being killed when IFP supporters rampaged through Kagiso township on the West Rand in May.

In June 1991, retired SADF colonel Nico Basson admitted that the government had covertly supplied assault weapons and other assistance to **Inkatha** in its fight to undermine and weaken the ANC. The allegations were denied by Mangosuthu Buthelezi.

Also in June, South Africa agreed to sign the **Nuclear Non-Proliferation Treaty**. Under this treaty South Africa permitted the inspection of its nuclear facilities. It was not until March 1993 that President F W de Klerk disclosed details of the government's covert nuclear weapons programme which started in 1974 in preparation against what was seen as a growing threat of communism in the sub-region.

In July the **International Olympic Committee (IOC)** removed its 23-year ban on South Africa recognising the Interim National Olympic Committee and paving the way for South Africa's re-entrance to the Olympic Games.

At around the same time the United States and several other countries such as Israel lifted **sanctions** which had been levied against South Africa. Various groups in South Africa argued that moves such as these were premature. Some countries like Denmark refused proposals to lift sanctions against South Africa. Several countries also re-established diplomatic relations with South Africa.

In the so-called '**Inkatha-gate**' scandal of July 1991, personal assistant to Buthelezi, M Z Khumalo, resigned after admitting to receiving funds from the Security police for Inkatha rallies. The government admitted to providing funds for the launch of an Inkatha-dominated union, the United Workers Union of South Africa (UWUSA).

In spite of the growing momentum of changes in legislation, various interest groups failed to halt offensive actions to defend their own personal interests. Among these groups were white right-wing organisations which continued to mobilise resistance in their ranks.

VENTERSDORP INCIDENT

A bloody confrontation between the security forces and members of the Afrikaner Weerstandbeweging (AWB) took place in August 1991 when State President F W de Klerk attended a meeting of the National Party at Ventersdorp, a stronghold of the Afrikaner Conservative Party (CP/KP). The AWB mobilised some 2 000 of its members to gatecrash the meeting, claiming that there were certain 'burning issues' they wanted to discuss with the president. In the ensuing confrontation with the police, three AWB members were killed and 58 people were injured. Nearly the entire AWB leadership was arrested on charges of public violence.

1991

In August 1991 **Ismael Mahomed** became the first black judge to be appointed to the Supreme Court of South Africa.

In September, the government, the ANC, the IFP and other major organisations signed the **National Peace Accord** to help re-establish peace in South Africa. The Accord made provision for a code of conduct for all the players in the conflict, including the police. It created a National Peace Committee and charged Justice Richard Goldstone with responsibility for enquiring into and monitoring the implementation of the agreement.

In October, nearly a hundred organisations met in Durban at the **Patriotic Front** conference and called for the establishment of a sovereign interim government or transitional authority pending democratic elections and the adoption of a new constitution.

In December 1991 the first group of **exiles** returned to South Africa under an agreement reached between the government and the United National High Commission for Refugees (UNHCR) which made provision for their indemnity from prosecution.

Author **Nadine Gordimer** (1923 –) won the Nobel Prize for literature in recognition of her powerful indictment of the apartheid system through a series of award-winning works of fiction including *The Conservationist* (1974) for which she won the Booker Prize in 1973, and *Burger's Daughter*.

CONVENTION FOR A DEMOCRATIC SOUTH AFRICA (CODESA)

The Convention for a Democratic South Africa (CODESA) became the forum for a wide range of government and non-government interest groups to negotiate a new constitution and the transition to democracy in South Africa. While the process aimed to be fully inclusive, it was at first boycotted by the PAC on the militant left and the Conservative Party on the white right. The CP campaigned instead for the setting up of a volkstaat (white state). (In April 1992 the CP expelled one of its members, Koos van der Merwe, who had called for participation in Codesa.) Moreover, Mangosuthu Buthelezi also refused at first to attend because Zulu King Goodwill Zwelethini had been left out.

The process was protracted and saw many heated exchanges. Trust-building between the role-players was hampered by continuing conflict in the country and widely-held suspicion that the security forces and government surrogates played a part in fomenting the violence. In March 1992 it was estimated that 11 000 people had been killed in political violence since 1986. Many monitoring agencies claimed that the violence besetting the country was the result of forces working to destabilise the democratic process. A Goldstone enquiry into the violence reported no evidence of a 'third force' but held the government responsible for its failure to act against criminal conduct in the security forces themselves. It held both the ANC and the IFP responsible for resorting to violence to secure territorial control.

In fits and starts the Codesa process proceeded, divided into five working groups, each charged with discussing an aspect of democratic governance. The process was frequently beset by disagreements and petty squabbling, mostly on questions of procedure, the protection of minority rights and the National Party's insistence on political and administrative control of the transition.

Codesa was dissolved in the middle of 1992 when parties fell out over the continuing and escalating violence in the country. The ANC pulled out of the talks, threatening country-wide mass action after over forty of its supporters were killed by hostel-dwellers in Boipatong. A general strike to protest against police collusion in the violence had a crippling effect on the country.

Against the backdrop of these talks, **political violence** raged in the East Rand townships, populated predominantly by migrant workers, and in Natal (later known as KwaZulu-Natal) where ANC and IFP supporters competed for political dominance. White **right-wing extremists** engaged in campaigns of sabotage and disruption in an attempt to abort the negotiating process. At the same time, **black extremists**, notably in APLA, carried out a series of attacks on civilians, principally on whites frequenting churches, clubs and other meeting places.

A PROTRACTED PEOPLE'S WAR

In the early 1990s, the PAC proclaimed a military strategy of 'protracted people's war', which involved the infiltration of APLA guerrillas into the country to conduct rural guerrilla warfare. The initial targets of such attacks were members of the security forces and white farmers who were perceived to be the frontline of defence for the former apartheid government.

A 'repossession unit' was also set up in which APLA cells conducted armed robberies on the instructions of the APLA High Command to raise funds and/ or obtain weapons and vehicles to enable APLA to carry out its military strategy. Many such robberies resulted in the killing and injuring of civilians.

In 1992 and 1993, attacks on civilians increased sharply with a series of high-profile attacks by APLA cadres on public places in urban areas usually, but not always, frequented by white civilians. These included restaurants, hotels and bars. The PAC/APLA claimed that the attacks were not racist in character, but directed against the apartheid government as all whites, according to the PAC, were complicit in the policy of apartheid. The 1993 attack on the St James' Church, Kenilworth, Cape Town, produced the highest number of casualties, with 11 people dead and 58 injured.

1992

In March the government held a **referendum** – for whites only – to determine their support for the aims of the Codesa process and requesting a mandate to proceed with constitutional reform. Nearly 70% of whites voted in favour of the process which would bring an end to white minority rule.

In June 1992, a delegation from the **International Commission of Jurists** toured the country. In their report they criticised IFP leader Mangosuthu Buthelezi for 'carrying a heavy responsibility for the escalation of violence'.

THE BOIPATONG MASSACRE

As many as 40 people died and 27 others were seriously injured on 17 June 1992 when IFP-supporting residents of the KwaMadala hostel launched attacks on residents in Boipatong, near Johannesburg. Victims included at least nine children, two babies and 17 women, one of whom was pregnant. Residents were raped, hacked, stabbed, shot, beaten and disembowelled. Police allegedly aided the hostel-dwellers in the attack. The ANC claimed that police forcibly removed residents patrolling the area in anticipation of the attack and were later seen escorting groups of the attackers. In a report under the auspices of the Goldstone Commission, Dr Peter Waddington said he found no evidence of police collusion in the killings but criticised the police force for its 'serious organisational problems'. Following the massacre the ANC suspended talks with the government and its participation in Codesa.

Efforts to put Codesa back on track came from many quarters both at home and abroad. In August 1992, the ANC mobilised workers in a country-wide

general strike to demand an end to the violence and for the installation of an interim government before the end of the year.

UN envoy **Cyrus Vance** visited the country and prepared a report for the Secretary-General on the violence and political stalemate in South Africa. In it he recommended that the role of the police and the army be investigated and called for the deployment of impartial foreign observers to work alongside the National Peace Secretariat in several identified 'flashpoints' in the country. Observers from the United Nations, the Organisation of African Unity (OAU), the Commonwealth and the European Union were despatched to the country.

Also in August 1992, the government and the ANC reached a joint '**Record of Understanding**' which paved the way for the resumption of negotiations. Agreement was reached on several contentious issues including the carrying of dangerous weapons and the isolation of a number of hostels throughout the country. It also laid down a timeframe for the transitional process.

IFP leader **Mangosuthu Buthelezi** expressed his opposition to the agreement saying that Zulu men would continue to carry cultural weapons. The IFP also released proposals for a constitutional monarchy in Natal (later known as KwaZulu-Natal), vigorously calling for regional autonomy.

BISHO MASSACRE

On 7 September 1992, the ANC, SACP and COSATU organised a march from King William's Town to the Ciskei capital of Bisho to demand free political activity in the homeland and the removal of the military ruler of the Ciskei, Brigadier Oupa Gqozo. Protesters had been prohibited by court order from entering Bisho. When part of the crowd tried to gain access to Bisho, Ciskei Defence Force (CDF) troops opened fire, killing 30 people, including one member of the CDF. Approximately 200 people were wounded in the shooting. In a report on the matter by the Goldstone Commission, the police shootings were condemned and criminal charges against those responsible were recommended. It also called for the censure of the ANC leaders responsible for leading the march and through provocation exposing their supporters to danger.

1992

In late September some political prisoners were released including **Robert McBride** (who had been responsible for the 1986 Magoo's Bar bomb), and right-winger **Barend Strydom** (responsible for the 1988 race killings in Pretoria), in line with the **Record of Understanding**. A further 42 political prisoners were released in November.

THE ASSASSINATION OF CHRIS HANI (1942 – 1993)

MK Chief of Staff and General Secretary of the SACP, Chris Hani was assassinated outside his home in Boksburg on 10 April 1993 by Janusz Waluz, a Polish immigrant. Hani had been among the most popular and influential political figures both in exile and at home during the transitional process. His death shocked the country to the core.

Waluz was arrested and charged with the killing, together with Clive Derby-Lewis, a Conservative Party member of the President's Council. Both were found guilty and received the death penalty, commuted to life sentences when the Constitutional Court declared capital punishment unconstitutional. Both men appealed to the Truth Commission for amnesty, citing the growing dissatisfaction of the right-wing Conservative Party with the reform process which peaked with the government's unbanning of political organisations in the country.

These reforms had led to a decision to take up arms to prevent the ANC/SACP alliance from plunging the country into communist misery and chaos. Many supporters of right-wing organisations interpreted the situation to be a call to the Afrikaner nation to take up arms in a fight for its freedom, and Chris Hani was regarded as public enemy no. 1.

The Amnesty Committee of the Truth Commission denied Walus and Derby-Lewis's applications on the grounds that the killing of Hani was not ordered by the Conservative Party, and not ratified or condoned after the fact.

1993

In April 1993, ANC president **Oliver Tambo** died after suffering a stroke.

NEGOTIATIONS BACK ON TRACK

Through an initiative of the government's Roelf Meyer (1947 –) and the ANC alliance's Cyril Ramaphosa (1952 –), the major stumbling blocks in the negotiations process were slowly overcome in private discussions. This led to the signing of a **Record of Understanding** aimed at a resumption of the negotiations process in April 1993. As players returned to the table, proposals made by SACP's Joe Slovo for the introduction of 'Sunset Clauses' made allowance for a coalition government for a fixed period with representation of the major parties at the highest level. The new round of negotiations was again boycotted by the Conservative Party and by Buthelezi who proposed a federal system of government to meet Zulu nationalist and royalist aspirations in Natal.

By the end of 1993, and in spite of continued political fighting, the multi-party conference reached agreement for the setting up of a multi-party **Transitional Executive Council (TEC)**. Consensus was reached on 27 constitutional principles and a bill of rights, and a date set for the first democratic election, scheduled for the following year.

1993

In October, F W de Klerk and Nelson Mandela were jointly awarded the **Nobel Peace Prize** in recognition for the role that each had played in bringing about a negotiated end to apartheid. A year earlier, they had each been awarded the Unesco Peace Prize.

In December 1993 the Transitional Executive Council (TEC) came into being with a mandate to ensure that the national elections would be free and fair. In the same month Nelson Mandela appealed to the United Nations to lift all remaining economic sanctions against the country. At the same time parliament approved the restoration of South African citizenship to residents of the homelands, estimated to be about 10 million people.

1994

As election year dawned, the country continued to be wracked by violence, not least perpetrated by disaffected members of the Afrikaner right-wing.

INVASION OF BOPHUTHATSWANA

On 11 March 1994 hundreds of AWB members drove into Bophuthatswana following a request for assistance from Chief Mangope to help restore control in the homeland, in the face of a strike by civil servants who demanded that the Mangope government introduce political reforms and adjust to the changing political circumstances in South Africa.

Under the leadership of AWB leader, Eugene Terre'Blanche, AWB members randomly attacked Mafikeng residents, killing 42 people. Three AWB members were shot dead by members of the Bophuthatswana Defence Force. Shortly after the incident and in a climate of widespread revolt, Chief Lucas Mangope was removed from power and a temporary administrator was put in his place by the TEC.

In March 1994 a revolt in the **Ciskei** police and defence forces resulted in the resignation of Brigadier Oupa Gqozo. As it had done in Bophuthatswana, the TEC installed a temporary administration in the territory.

In Johannesburg clashes broke out between IFP and ANC supporters on 28 March 1994 when IFP supporters staged a march to ANC headquarters at **Shell House**. ANC security guards, who claimed they were under attack, opened fire on the crowd from the building killing eight people and injuring nearly 100 others. Yet more people were killed and injured when the marchers returned to their homes in the evening.

During the pre-election period, the right-wing carried out a **sabotage campaign** aimed at derailing the electoral process and removing the National Party, in order to make it possible for them to move towards the creation of a Volkstaat by force. Public areas such as taxi ranks, bus stops and railway stations were targeted, as were private residential and business premises of those associated with the state, the ANC or the unfolding democratic order. On 24 and 25 April, 11 AWB members went on a bombing spree targeting black commuters. Twenty-six people died and over 40 were injured.

In Natal (later known as KwaZulu-Natal) fighting continued to rage between **ANC** and **IFP** supporters during the run-up to the 27 April election. A State of Emergency was declared in the province at the end of March in the hope of creating peaceful conditions for the election to take place.

Inkatha originally threatened to boycott the elections (as they had not participated in the Codesa talks). On 19 April, however, Chief Buthelezi was persuaded to participate and called upon his followers to attend the poll. Ballot papers had already been printed without listing the IFP as a contender. During the election, adhesive strips naming the IFP had to be stuck onto each individual ballot paper, at both national and provincial levels. With the IFP coming on board, a dramatic fall in the level of violence was experienced around the period of the election itself.

THE FIRST DEMOCRATIC ELECTION IN SOUTH AFRICA

Over 20 million eligible South Africans of all colours and persuasions went to the polls to cast their vote in the first democratic election from 27 – 29 April 1994. On polling days queues were to be seen snaking through the streets and paths of urban and rural South Africa. The mood was euphoric and voters, by far the majority of whom were voting for the very first time, were happy to wait long hours to cast their ballots. Amongst whites, rumours current before the elections forewarned of disaster and mayhem. Some stashed supplies and provisions in preparation for a siege. Their fears proved to be unfounded.

Nineteen political parties contested the election, among them the ANC, the PAC, the IFP, the National Party, the Democratic Party and the Freedom Front. At the polls voters cast two ballots, one for the national level of government and another for provincial government. The Independent Electoral Commission (IEC) hired over 10 000 observers to monitor the election.

In the election the ANC secured a landslide victory with 62.2% of the vote. The National Party received 20.39%, the IFP 10.43%, the Freedom Front 2.2%, the Democratic Party 1.7%, the PAC 1.2%, and the African Christian Democratic Party (ACDP) 0.5%.

At provincial level, the ANC won 7 out of 9 provinces, with the National Party taking the Western Cape and the IFP taking KwaZulu-Natal.

Head of the IEC, Justice Johan Kriegler announced that the elections had been "substantially free and fair". Although there had been technical flaws in the process, the result was a fair reflection of the will of the people.

1994

A new six-colour **national flag**, combining the colours of the old regime with the colours of diverse players in the struggle against apartheid, was flown for

the first time on 27 April 1994 and a new **national anthem**, *Nkosi Sikelel'
iAfrika* (Lord bless Africa) was introduced. Written by Enoch Sontonga in 1897,
the anthem had been sung at political and community meetings for decades
of struggle against discrimination and injustice in South Africa. A hundred
years after Sontonga wrote the words, the anthem was formally adopted and
included two verses, in English and Afrikaans, from *Die Stem*.

Nkosi sikelel' iAfrika
Nkosi sikelel' iAfrika
Maluphakanyisw' uphondo lwayo,
Yizwa imithandazo yethu,
Nkosi sikelela, thina lusapho lwayo.

Morena boloka setjhaba sa heso,
O fedise dintwa le matshwenyeho,
O se boloke, O se boloke setjhaba sa heso,
Setjhaba sa South Afrika – South Afrika.

Uit die blou van onse hemel,
Uit die diepte van onse see,
Oor ons ewige gebergtes,
Waar die kranse antwoord gee,

Sounds the call to come together,
And united we shall stand.
Let us live and strive for freedom,
In South Africa our land.

On 10 May 1994 **Nelson Mandela** was inaugurated as President of the
democratic Republic of South Africa. In his speech at the dazzling
inauguration ceremony attended by tens of thousands of people at the Union
Buildings in Pretoria, he said:

"*We enter into a covenant that we shall build a society in which all South
Africans, both black and white, will be able to walk tall, without any fear in
their hearts, assured of their inalienable right to human dignity – a rainbow
nation at peace with itself and the world.*"

CHAPTER 11

THE FIRST TEN YEARS OF DEMOCRACY

1994 – 2004

With Nelson Mandela as head of the new Government of National Unity, the new South Africa was instantly re-admitted to the world's stage as an equal partner. The country became a member of the Organisation of African Unity (OAU) and the Commonwealth. As an emblem of national reconciliation, Mandela himself had a vital role to play in encouraging all South Africans to make the new dispensation 'their own' and in encouraging international investment back to the country.

Mandela announced that the government of national unity would draw in those who remained in opposition. PAC members were brought into government structures. Former APLA cadres were incorporated into the re-formed South African National Defence Force (SANDF).

The new order reflected some advance for the rights of women, who made up a third of elected parliamentarians and saw the appointment of Dr Frene Ginwala as speaker.

The first years of democratic rule in South Africa presented the government and the people with the challenge of transforming society into one which reflected the values enshrined in the new constitution. This would be no easy task. The state would need to institutionalise a process by which individuals and groups in the country, formerly sworn enemies, could be reconciled. It would need to confront the past and find ways to heal the wounds of a divided society.

A NEW CONSTITUTION

After the inauguration of the new government, Cyril Ramaphosa and Roelf Meyer continued to facilitate the constitution-building process. As co-chairpersons of the Constitutional Assembly they encouraged South Africans from all spheres of society to make submissions to the process and by the beginning of 1997, after a few revisions, the new Constitution was adopted by parliament.

The new constitution, seen by many as one of the most progressive charters in the world, gives due recognition to the right of all individuals to equality and integrity and extends these rights to the recognition of the rights of groups. Eleven official languages (Afrikaans, English, Ndebele, North Sotho, Seswati, Sesotho, Tsonga, Setswana, Venda, isiXhosa and isiZulu) are given equal recognition and groups have the rights, where this is practical, to education and legal counsel in their mother-tongue. The nine provinces of South Africa (**KwaZulu-Natal**, Northern Transvaal (later the Northern Province, then the **Limpopo Province**), the **North-West Province**, the PWV (later **Gauteng**), **Mpumalanga**, the Orange Free State (later the **Free State**), the **Western Cape**, the **Eastern Cape** and the **Northern Cape** are each administered by an elected regional administration, centrally controlled by a National Council of Provinces. An elected National Assembly acts as parliament on terms of no more than five years.

The new Constitution made possible the termination of pregnancy and also, in June 1995, the Constitutional Court formally abolished the death penalty, following the moratorium on all hangings announced by F W de Klerk in February 1990. Unless the Constitution is re-written (only permissible by a party who secures a two-thirds electoral majority) it cannot be overturned.

The new government faced a daunting task with substantial development needed in all aspects of life in South Africa: health, education, transport, welfare, housing, land distribution and urban renewal. Several countries announced multi-million dollar aid packages for the government-sponsored schemes in reconstruction and development of the country, and for the upliftment of the 'previously disadvantaged' majority.

THE RECONSTRUCTION AND DEVELOPMENT PROGRAMME (RDP)

Based on the ANC's election manifesto *A Better Life For All*, the Reconstruction and Development Programme aimed to redistribute land, to create jobs, to provide housing, electricity, sanitation, health care and free education for 10 years. Authorities and structures in the government were set up to administer the programme and some initial success was had in reaching its ambitious goals. In 1997, under Thabo Mbeki's leadership of the programme, private enterprise was co-opted in an effort to accelerate delivery in providing education, health care, shelter and basic services. By 1999 the RDP had reached 75% of its original target for the provision of new homes. Substantial advances had been made in the provision of electricity and water to rural and peri-urban communities.

However, the RDP also experienced various set-backs. Developed within a conservative financial framework and at a time of slump in the gold price, the economy struggled to muster competencies equal to a global economy. Unemployment persisted unrelieved, skills-development in the labour economy suffered from serious deficiencies and skilled professionals continued to stream out of the country in search of better pastures.

Because of the change in government, many overseas funders who had given money to Non-Government Organisations (NGO's) now gave their money directly to the RDP and other government projects. The number of NGOs declined dramatically, and many of their employees were now employed by the government.

1995

Compulsory schooling was introduced in January for all children between the ages of five and 14.

1995

In November **local government elections** were held, bringing around 5.3 million people to the polls (51.37% voter participation). The ANC scored an overall victory with 66.37% of votes cast. Local elections in both the Western Cape and KwaZulu-Natal were postponed.

In 1995, the national South African **football** team, Bafana Bafana (the boys), won the African Nations Cup. The Springbok **rugby** team won the Rugby World Cup on home ground. Nelson Mandela attended the cup final in Johannesburg wearing a Springbok rugby jersey which produced a surge in feelings of optimism for reconciliation in South Africa.

On the understanding that unless South Africans address the brutality of its apartheid past, there could be no hope for the future, in 1995 the Promotion of National Unity and Reconciliation Act No 34 was passed, bringing into being the **Truth and Reconciliation Commission (TRC)**.

THE TRUTH AND RECONCILIATION COMMISSION (TRC)

Headed by Archbishop Desmond Tutu, the TRC was charged with the task of promoting reconciliation and unity in South Africa by looking into and providing as complete a picture as possible of the nature, causes and extent of gross violations of human rights committed during the years of apartheid (1960 – 1994).

The Commission comprised three committees: a Human Rights Violations Committee which called for victims of apartheid to come forward with their accounts of suffering; an Amnesty Committee which called for perpetrators to come forward with accounts of the acts for which they were entitled to apply for amnesty; and a Reparations Committee which could make recommendations to the government for the award of appropriate recompense to victims of human rights violations.

In a series of cathartic public hearings, the Commission heard testimony from a wide range of people – both opponents and defenders of the apartheid system.

Some refused to co-operate with the process, notably former State President P W Botha who declared he would never apologise for apartheid, and IFP leader, Mangosuthu Buthelezi who until late in the day encouraged his supporters to boycott the process.

Throughout and since its existence, the TRC elicited a welter of mixed feelings. While the majority of South Africans supported the process, some felt that it opened old wounds. Many whites opposed the process, refusing to believe the accounts of apartheid atrocities. Some refused to accept the Act's provision for a relatively low burden of proof in establishing the occurrence of alleged events. The Truth Commission made findings on the 'balance of probability' and not 'beyond reasonable doubt' as in law.

In 1998 the Commission published a five-volume report summarising its work and making findings. The report was criticised by the ANC who argued that there was no moral equivalence in the violations committed by former members of the security forces and violations committed by members of liberation movements in exile.

It also alienated the Inkatha Freedom Party for its stinging indictment of IFP members involved in political violence of the 1980s and 1990s in both KwaZulu-Natal and the East Rand. In 2001 IFP leader, Mangosuthu Buthelezi, brought proceedings before the High Court to restrain the Commission from publishing its final two volumes and a report on the work of the Amnesty Committee, demanding that negative findings on the IFP be expunged from the report. While the decision of the court permitted several cosmetic changes to the 1998 report, and granted the IFP permission to publish a minority opinion in the 2001 report, the Commission's core findings on the IFP remained unchanged.

The TRC recommended that the state erect 'Lest-we-forget' symbols and monuments to project and exalt the freedom struggle. It further recommended that medical, education, and housing benefits be made available for the rehabilitation of certain communities. The Commission recommended also a sliding scale of cash payments to the 22 000 applicants who were found to have been victims of gross violations. In 2003 the government announced that a once-off payment of R30 000 would be made to victims. It also announced that there would be no general amnesty, leaving the way open for civil prosecutions to be brought against perpetrators who failed to co-operate with the amnesty process.

ARCHBISHOP DESMOND TUTU

Anglican Archbishop Emeritus Desmond Mpilo Tutu (1931 –), who was awarded the Nobel Peace Prize in 1984, was an outspoken and passionate critic of apartheid. He played a leading and prophetic role in the fight for democracy and justice in South Africa. After his retirement as Archbishop of Cape Town, he was appointed to head the Truth and Reconciliation Commission. Tutu stood firmly by the Commission's report which castigated organisations and individuals across the board for a range of human rights abuses.

In 1998 he took sabbatical leave in the United States. He was diagnosed with prostate cancer at around this time and has had several bouts of treatment for it. In relatively good health today, he continues to be a powerful spiritual leader and agent for peace and reconciliation in South Africa.

1996

National **crime statistics** released in 1996 gave rise to the designation of the country as 'the most violent country outside a war zone'. South Africans were spending more and more of their disposable incomes on security measures to protect their homes, cars and lives.

With a resurgence of the **political conflict** in KwaZulu-Natal, President Mandela met with Zulu King Goodwill Zwelethini and Mangosuthu Buthelezi to plan an *imbizo* (Zulu traditional gathering) to discuss ways of ending the conflict. In March a large group of IFP supporters attended a rally in the Tugela Ferry district of the province – carrying traditional weapons in defiance of a government ban on carrying weapons in public. IFP supporters in Johannesburg marched in the same month to commemorate the Shell House shootings of 1994, and also carried traditional weapons in defiance of the ruling. A year later, during another commemorative march to Shell House, police responded with force to an eruption of violence. Three people were killed and several others wounded.

In March 1996, the **Human Rights Commission** was established by the government and charged with the task of investigating human rights abuses and implementing a human rights culture in South Africa.

1996

In April, South Africa signed the **African Nuclear Weapon Free Zone Treaty** in Cairo.

In June, the **National Party** withdrew from the Government of National Unity moving into parliamentary opposition. Most of the NP appointees to the cabinet were replaced with ANC appointees. The NP also withdrew from all provincial governments, except the Western Cape where it enjoyed a majority. In local elections held in the Western Cape at the end of May, the National Party maintained its majority.

In June, Trevor Manuel, now Minister of Finance, unveiled the **Growth, Employment and Redistribution (GEAR)** policy framework for macro-economic development. This moved away from the welfarist principles of the Freedom Charter and the RDP, and was criticised by many left-wing academics and civil society groups for its emphasis on foreign investment and the free market, and its neglect of issues of wealth redistribution and service provision.

Also in June, **local elections** were held in KwaZulu-Natal. The IFP secured 44.5% of the vote, the ANC 33.2%. While the IFP took control of most of the province's rural councils, the ANC won control of all 13 metropolitan councils. The poll was declared largely free and fair in spite of complaints of administrative bungles and intimidation.

In August, 1996, an alleged drug dealer, Rashaad Staggie was shot and burnt to death during a march organised by **PAGAD (People Against Gangsterism and Drugs)**, a Muslim organisation established to combat crime in local communities in Cape Town.

In August, the Supreme Court in Pretoria convicted **Colonel Eugene de Kock**, a former member of the security police, on several counts of murder arising from his time as head of Vlakplaas, a secret police unit located outside Pretoria. Giving testimony to the court, he revealed details of the former regime's campaign of 'dirty tricks' incriminating leading political figures and members of the security forces. Former President F W de Klerk told the Truth Commission that the National Party government had never, to his knowledge, authorised the security forces to commit unlawful acts including torture and murder of political activists. De Kock was sentenced twice to life imprisonment for murder and conspiracy to murder.

THE 'MALAN' TRIAL

Former Minister of Defence, General Magnus Malan, stood trial with 19 others on charges of murder in the so-called 'KwaMakhutha massacre'. The accused ranged from senior-ranking members of the former security forces and the SADF, to an IFP official and ordinary IFP supporters.

On 21 January 1987, 13 people, mostly women and children, were killed when gunmen opened fire with AK47s on the home of UDF activist, Mr Bheki Ntuli, at KwaMakhutha, Amanzimtoti, near Durban. Mr Ntuli was not at home at the time.

Malan and all of his co-accused, who included IFP leader, M Z Khumalo, were acquitted in the Durban Supreme Court in 1996 for their part in an alleged conspiracy between former state structures and the IFP to carry out the attack. Information about the conspiracy emanated from former defence force members who confessed to playing a part in the so-called Operation Marion in which the SADF Military Intelligence's Special Tasks provided paramilitary training and support to the IFP in a joint effort to combat the revolutionary threat posed by the ANC.

In November 1996, faced with charges of **corruption** and **nepotism**, the Free State Premier, Patrick 'Terror' Lekota and his executive committee resigned en bloc. Ivy Matsepe-Casaburri was installed as Provincial Premier in Lekota's place and Lekota took a place in national government.

1996

South Africans have always shared an enthusiasm and fervour for **sport**. While in the past, this was played out in separate arenas, the new democracy brought a great surge of support for our national teams and our national sporting heroes.

For the first time since 1960, South Africans participated in the **Olympic Games** in Atlanta. Penny Heyns brought home double gold for her victories in the 100 m and 200 m breaststroke. Marianne Kriel was awarded a bronze medal in the 100 m backstroke and Hezekiel Sepeng won a silver medal in the men's 800 m. Josiah Thugwane won the Olympic marathon in the closest finish in Olympic history. Six months before the Games, Thugwane had been shot in the face by hijackers.

1997

When Mandela opened parliament in February 1997, he announced a governmental programme of action in the **fight against crime** which had risen to alarming proportions. National Police Commissioner, George Fivaz, and Minister of Safety and Security, Sydney Mufamadi, were appointed to a special team to combat crime from the highest level.

The value of the **Rand** took a dive in response to the economic crisis in Asia. It fell from around R8 to almost R20 to the British sterling within a few years, and recovered to around R12 by 2003.

President Nelson Mandela retired from his position of ANC president, handing over to **Thabo Mbeki**. Mandela said he would not stand for re-election in 1999. At around this time, his former wife, Winnie Madikizela-Mandela, was summoned to give evidence before the TRC on the alleged activities of the Mandela United Football Team.

The year saw a number of **realignments in party politics** with top level resignations from the IFP (including that of KZN Premier Frank Mdlalose), and the forming of the United Democratic Alliance (UDM) by former homeland leader, Bantu Holomisa, and former National Party MP, Roelf Meyer. The National Party itself entered talks with the IFP, the Democratic Party and others about establishing a broad oppositional political front.

In April, realignment in the **labour sector** saw the establishment of the new Federation of Unions of South Africa (FEDUSA) which claimed a membership of over half a million people in 25 affiliated unions.

Also in April the **Council of Traditional Leaders** was inaugurated in parliament. Present at the ceremony were the kings of Lesotho and Swaziland.

1997

In the **golfing** arena, Ernie Els won the US Open for the second time, repeating his victory in 1994. He became the first foreign player in 90 years to win the event twice. A year later, Ernie Els and the South African team won the Dunhill Cup.

1998

During a period when President Mandela was overseas, Dr Mangosuthu Buthelezi as acting President authorised a defence force invasion of **Lesotho** to quell an army mutiny in that country. The operation was brief and successful in maintaining the leadership of the government of the time.

Nelson Mandela married **Graça Machel**, the widow of the former President of Mozambique, Samora Machel, who had allegedly been assassinated by apartheid forces in the 1980s.

1999

In the second national democratic election, the ANC again scored a **landslide victory** although it narrowly failed to gain a two-thirds majority. Thabo Mbeki was inaugurated as President. The compulsory coalition of the parties fell away. However, the ANC entered into a coalition with IFP to secure stability in KwaZulu-Natal. The Democratic Party (later renamed the Democratic Alliance) became the official opposition with an increase to 38 in its number of parliamentary seats. The New National Party won only 28 seats. The DP and the NNP entered into coalition in the Western Cape to keep the ANC out of power provincially.

By the end of the 90s, questions of crime, corruption in high places and the HIV and AIDS epidemic were uppermost on the nation-building agenda. Political leaders met at a summit in 1998 to discuss the idea of 'moral regeneration' in the nation and Thabo Mbeki began to advocate the idea of an 'African renaissance' to lift Africa out of poverty and its marginalised position in the global village. The new millennium, he said, would see the dawn of an 'African century'.

2000

In July, the 13th **International AIDS Conference** was held in Durban. Twelve-year-old Nkosi Johnson, who had become the human face of the epidemic in South Africa and a mobilising force in the fight against HIV and AIDS, addressed the gathering. Nkosi died in 2001.

HIV AND AIDS

From 2000 HIV and AIDS in South Africa presented a fundamental crisis in the country. The turn of the millennium saw the rapid rise of public awareness campaigns on the escalating HIV and AIDS problem in the country. These, however, could do little to reverse the social and economic problems brought about by a critically high infection rate and the resulting assault on worker productivity and on millions of ordinary households, many already afflicted with dire poverty.

Researchers estimated that by 2003, nearly 5 million South Africans were HIV-positive, giving South Africa one of the highest infection rates in the world. Between 600 and 1 000 people die every day from AIDS-related illnesses.

HIV and AIDS has had a substantial impact on the status of women and children in South Africa. By 2001, there were already estimated to be up to 3 million children orphaned by the deaths of parents, breadwinners and primary care-givers. Furthermore, the myth of 'virgin-cleansing' brought a substantial increase in the incidence of rape and female child abuse across the country. Women, who are biologically and culturally more vulnerable to HIV infection in South Africa, also bare the brunt of AIDS stigmatisation in conservative and deeply frightened local communities.

As more and more people in South Africa became infected and affected by HIV and AIDS, the government and various organisations adopted radically different points of view about the causes and possible responses to the pandemic.

In 2002 President Thabo Mbeki was pilloried for his opposition to the provision of AIDS drugs in South Africa when he argued that these are dangerously toxic and suggested that poverty was the true cause of the AIDS pandemic. The President and the Minister of Health weathered strong international criticism for their 'denialist' stance on the AIDS problem. At home the **Treatment Action Campaign** (TAC) led the way in pressurising the government to alter its stance and begin to roll-out anti-retroviral treatment for millions of infected South Africans. At a meeting of the cabinet in August 2003, a national treatment plan for HIV and AIDS sufferers was adopted.

The government reversal has come late in the day and it remains to be seen whether implementation of a changed government policy will substantially alter the fact that up to 60% of infections world-wide occur in sub-Saharan Africa.

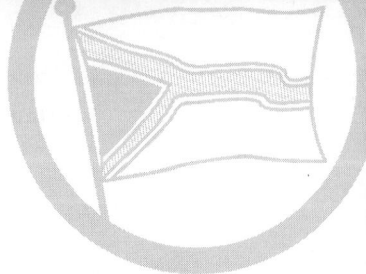

2000

Floods in neighbouring Mozambique devastated the country. The South African National Defence Force (SANDF) mounted a massive rescue operation, gaining international applause.

In the same year **PAGAD** was held to blame for up to 20 bomb explosions in the City of Cape Town. Several of its leaders were arrested and convicted.

The cabinet agreed to a strategic defence package which involved the purchase of the largest ever consignment of arms for the security forces and the expenditure of up to R50 billion. Allegations of bribery and 'kick-backs' plagued the deal, implicating – amongst others – Deputy President Jacob Zuma. An official enquiry into the **arms deal** did not, however, establish corruption on a significant scale.

South Africans, **Monique and Callie Strydom** were released after four months in captivity on the Philippines island of Jolo, after being taken hostage with other tourists.

Cricket captain, Hansie Cronje, admitted before the King Commission that he had fixed matches in return for bribes from Indian bookmakers. The United Cricket Board moved to ban Cronje for life. Two years later Cronje was killed tragically in an air crash near George.

2001

In April, 43 people were killed in a stampede at **Ellis Park** stadium, Johannesburg, during a soccer match between Kaizer Chiefs and Orlando Pirates. While 60 000 people had been admitted to the stadium, a further 15 000 failed to get tickets. After a goal was scored during the match, thousands of soccer supporters outside pushed their way into the stadium, trampling those in front of them. Over a hundred people were injured.

2002

In neighbouring **Zimbabwe**, the Zanu PF-led government of Robert Mugabe continued to condone, and even promote the seizure of white-owned farmland by party supporters. At home, President Mbeki came under increasing pressure for his refusal to condemn the land invasions and to censure Robert Mugabe, adopting instead a policy of quiet diplomacy towards the embattled president of South Africa's northern neighbour.

Baby Jake Matlala defeated the Colombian Juan Herrera in the WBU junior flyweight **boxing championship**. Baby Jake is the only South African to have won four world titles.

As the new millennium established itself, many South Africans continued to score 'firsts' in feats of endurance, skill and talent. Internet millionaire, **Mark Shuttleworth**, joined a Russian space team to visit the International Space Station. A South African team summited **Everest**.

2003

South African born actress, Charlize Theron, won an **Oscar** for her performance in the film 'Monster'.

A few defeats, some sensational, were to follow the country's triumphant re-entry into the world sporting arenas.

With South Africa as host nation for the **Cricket World Cup**, the Proteas suffered a withering defeat on the field, losing in the opening group stages to the West Indies, New Zealand and Sri Lanka. The Springboks were resoundingly defeated by New Zealand in the quarter final of the **Rugby World Cup**.

2003

In 2003 also, former Minister of Transport, Mac Maharaj, accused the Director of the National Prosecuting Authority (or 'Scorpions'), Bulelani Ngcuka of having been a spy during the apartheid era. **Justice Joos Hefer** was ordered to investigate the claim in a commission of enquiry. He found the allegations to be without substance.

The affair arose out of the Public Prosecutor's statement that Deputy President Jacob Zuma was under investigation for allegedly profiting from favourable tender awards in the government's **arms procurement programme**.

The country became mesmerised by the story of **Happy Sindane** who claimed to be a white child, kidnapped from his home and raised in a rural black community. After investigation, it was established that Happy, whose real name is Abbey Mzayiya, was the child of a black woman and a white man. A well-known paint company came under fire for using the image of Happy Sindane in an advertising campaign, under the slogan of 'Any colour you want'.

2004

The country rejoiced when it was announced in May that South Africa was to host the **World Cup Soccer** in 2010. This is yet another indication of a move towards international inclusion, and recognition of the miracle that has taken place in the last 10 years.

TEN YEARS OF DEMOCRACY IN SOUTH AFRICA

On 14 April 2004, ten years after the birth of democracy, South Africans again went to the polls in a national and provincial **general election**. While many people predicted that voters would stay away from the polls in apathy, 15 million voters, of the 20 million eligible citizens on the voters roll, turned out to vote.

The election was described 'free and fair' and the electoral process as professional and competent. After the votes were counted, it was clear that the ruling ANC had polled just under 70% of the vote and had secured a two-thirds majority.

In KwaZulu-Natal the Inkatha Freedom Party lost to the ANC, in spite of a coalition with the Democratic Alliance.

The New National Party suffered a humiliating defeat and remained with token representation in the National Assembly. The NNP leader was, however, offered a portfolio in Mbeki's cabinet.

With around 12.4% of the vote, the Democratic Alliance had suffered a setback but continues as official parliamentary opposition. The Independent Democrats, formed by Patricia de Lille following her departure from the PAC, had a noteworthy showing in the results, many disaffected supporters from the other established political parties opting to support her instead.

In 2004, the tenth anniversary of democracy in South Africa saw the opening of the Constitutional Court in Johannesburg. Situated on 'Constitutional Hill', the impressive building is a beacon of the infant democracy. It has been built alongside the Fort, a former prison notorious for the brutal treatment of thousands of political activists and awaiting trial prisoners during the years of apartheid.

South Africans have themselves to applaud for the achievements and triumphs of the first ten years of democracy. Transforming South African society has not been an easy task. Neither is it over. Nelson Mandela taught us this:

[1]*"I have walked that long road to freedom. I have tried not to falter; I have made missteps along the way. But I have discovered the secret that after climbing a great hill, one only finds that there are many more hills to climb. I have taken a moment here to rest, to steal a view of the glorious vista that surrounds me, to look back on the distance I have come. But I can rest only for a moment, for with freedom comes responsibilities, and I dare not linger, for my long walk is not yet ended."*

[1] Mandela, Nelson: *Long Walk To Freedom*, p. 751

CHAPTER 12

THE SECOND POST-DEMOCRACY DECADE

2005

HIV/Aids: By this stage around 28 per cent of the population of South Africa was thought to have been affected by this pandemic, with an estimated 365 000 people having died from the disease as a and its consequences due to the denial of the causes of HIV by President Mbeki and the lack of a strategic approach to treatment. A large-scale antiretroviral treatment programme was implemented in South Africa around this time, initially supported by the US Presidents Emergency Plan for AIDS relief.

The President, Thabo Mbeki, seemed to support controversial neighbour, Robert Mugabe, President of Zimbabwe. In the **Zimbabwe elections of 2005**, South Africa sent a foreign observer mission to oversee the elections but the official reports of "peaceful, credible and well mannered elections" were disputed by opposition both in Zimbabwe and in South Africa, and included allegations of violent intimidation and fraud in the tallying of votes.

2006

The South African Constitution provides for freedom of sexual orientation as an inalienable human right. This cause was further promoted in November 2006 when South Africa became the **first African country to legalise same-sex marriage**, on a continent where gay and lesbian rights are largely absent.

2007

In December 2007, the Polokwane Conference of the ANC, to the surprise of some executive members, **chose Jacob Zuma to succeed Thabo Mbeki** as the Presidential candidate for the 2009 elections. Zuma was supported by a new voice in South African politics – that of Julius Malema.

TRANSPORT ISSUES
Congestion on the roads of Gauteng led the government to introduce three initiatives to solve the problems on the roads and to lessen the time spent travelling.

Rea Vaya, a bus rapid-transport system, was introduced in the Johannesburg area amid protests from the taxi industry.

Construction on the Gautrain, a fast train service between Pretoria, Johannesburg and OR Tambo airport, was started in 2006, and the first phase opened in 2012. It has proved very popular with commuters.

The South African National Roads Agency (SANRAL) undertook a roads improvement programme on the main roads around Gauteng province, called **the Gauteng Freeway Improvement Project (GFIP)**. The collection of toll fees, in an electronic system which is the largest in the world, has become a highly vexed issue. Revenue for the road improvements was raised from investors all over the world, and is to be paid back through the collection of toll fees through the use of gantry collection points working on electronic tags fitted to vehicles. Many organisations and individuals have refused to comply with these demands which are seen as illegitimate, and the system is still not fully operational in 2015.

OUTA is one organisation defying the tolling of these roads on the user-pays principle, and they are joined by several other organisations and unions, as well as sections of the taxi and other industries.

President Mbeki at this stage was not only debating the causes of the HIV/AIDS pandemic, but was claiming that reports of violent crime by the African Peer Review Mechanism (APRM) were exaggerated. The APRM found that South Africa had the world's second highest murder rate.

2008
Xenophobic attacks took place in early 2008, leading to more than 40 deaths, the injuries of hundreds and the displacement of thousands of foreigners, mainly Zimbabweans, who were blamed for unemployment, crime and housing shortages. These Zimbabweans had come to South Africa to escape the economic trials in Zimbabwe at the start of the international financial collapse.

To add to the trials of the President and government, it became obvious that the anticipated rate of growth in South Africa had been underestimated, and it became necessary to **limit power usage** by turning off Eskom power countrywide in scheduled **rolling 'black-outs'.** This affected the mining and other industries and cost the country billions of rands in economic losses.

In September, **Thabo Mbeki resigned** after serving nearly two terms as President. He was recalled by the ANC Executive Committee after allegations of political interference into the case against the Deputy President Jacob Zuma. He was succeeded by **Kgalema Motlanthe**, an ANC MP who replaced Mbeki for the remainder of the term until the 2009 elections. The political situation within the ANC Youth League continued to be controversial with the election of **Julius Malema as President**, winning a narrow margin over Saki Mofokeng, in a situation of obvious intimidation and fraud. Malema was elected unopposed for a second term in 2011 and went on to become one of the most controversial figures in South African politics.

President Mbeki intervened in the critical situation in Zimbabwe, and brokered a deal between ZANU-PF and opposition parties in which Morgan Tsvangirai became Prime Minister and Mugabe remained President. One of the largest groups yet to split from the ANC, the Congress of the People (COPE), was formed with the intention of contesting the 2009 elections. The party gained substantial support in the Eastern Cape, but infighting saw factions develop and, after a strong showing in 2009, COPE was almost obliterated from the political scene by the 2014 elections.

2009

The **crime rate** in South Africa continued to be worrying with the number of murders reported at over 18 000 in 2009, similar to the number of road deaths. The private security industry had become the largest in the world with nearly half a million registered active private security guards, outnumbering the combined police and army.

Sexually based crimes continued to be prevalent, including rape of lesbians as a 'cure' for their orientation, and child and baby rape often owing to the belief that sex with a virgin cures HIV/AIDS. This continues to cause outrage and these tragedies still occur.

The Deputy President, **Jacob Zuma, was suspended** from his post in the wake of allegations of corruption and racketeering, as well as his pending rape trial. In April 2009 corruption charges against him were dropped, many believing this due political interference by Mbeki.

On 9 May Zuma was inaugurated as the fourth post-apartheid President of South Africa. Soon after his inauguration a security assessment was carried out of his **private residence in Nkandla**, and the upgrades, later to become very controversial, were begun in August.

CORRUPTION IN SOUTH AFRICA

The new South Africa has been proud of its free press, and editors and journalists continue to play their role in bringing to the attention of the public the fraudulent activities which are so prevalent in the country. Increasing pressure on the press to 'self regulate' their criticism of the government, particularly of the President, first became obvious around 2010, after the media had highlighted various corrupt activities of government including the state's expenditure on the Nkandla upgrade.

With the decentralisation of government authority since 1994, corrupt administration by the provinces and local authorities was estimated to cost the country R30 billion annually (2012-2013 figures), in spite of the existence of about 35 state organisations whose role is to curb corruption. A new bureau, formed in 2013, aimed to identify fraudulent and corrupt activities and to protect whistle-blowers. Its efficacy is still to be judged.

The Office of the Public Protector, under the leadership of Thuli Madonsela, continues to investigate areas of corruption including the spending on the private residence of Jacob Zuma at Nkandla. The office of the Auditor General, under Terence Nombembe, also identified many areas of illegal and fraudulent expenditure, but little appears to have been done to recover the money or punish those responsible. Both of these leadership positions are limited by the Constitution, and the new leadership may not have the commitment and courage of those who serve currently.

The Judiciary, Parliament, the National Prosecuting Authority, the Special Investigation Unit, the Human Rights Commission and other state bodies should also have a role to play in this regard, but operate at various levels of political independence and integrity themselves. *"Let me stress again that the elephant in the room is none other than the President. There is a cloud that hangs over Zuma and has done so ever since he was first accused of fraud and corruption"* – Alex Boraine.

When the ANC recognises the fact that Jacob Zuma is more of an embarrassment than an asset, then progress may be made against corrupt activities. Until then, the continued corruption and lack of honesty and integrity in the appointments of public officers in contracts and tenders and in sheer theft will contribute to the downward slide to 'a failed state'.

Corruption Watch is an independent non-profit organisation and received 4000 reports in its first 15 months of operations. They hope to highlight government corruption in the public service and in schools particularly.

2010

South Africa was the first country in Africa to be chosen to hold the **FIFA soccer world cup**. The competition involved 32 competing teams who played at nine venues throughout the country, especially built or upgraded for this competition. The competition was highly successful, and the anticipated security problems proved groundless with most of the millions of visitors visiting the country and attending the matches in safety. Spain was the winner, taking away $30 million in prize money, and boasting rights for the next four years. South Africa is still liable for the billions of rands spent on road upgrades and the building and improvements to the stadiums.

In the background, the **Nkandla homestead security upgrades** continued to be built, with progress reports being given to the President on the cattle culvert, a perimeter fence, inner high security fence, guard house, tuck shop, refuse and electrical rooms, electrical supply, sewerage treatment plant, relocation of families, upgrade of water supply, helipad, excavation for clinic, entrance bypass, services to park homes and the bunker, as well as soccer fields and various other building unrelated to security. Details of these upgrades became public in 2011 as the result of a story in a national newspaper, and remain controversial.

The **Decade of Action for Road Safety** (2010-2020) was launched in Gauteng, as a response to international pressure to reduce the carnage on roads, particularly in developing countries. The aim was to reduce fatalities by 50 per cent, but little has been achieved by 2014.

2011

Strategic partnerships with China strengthened during this year, and many South African government officials visited China as part of the 'comprehensive strategic partnership' agreements. In April South Africa became part of the **BRIC grouping of countries** (Brazil, Russia, India and China), which were seen as the largest trading partners of both South Africa and Africa.

The **Nkandla issue** again hit the headlines at this time, with upgrade cost estimates of R65 million to be paid by the taxpayer. Government denied any role in the upgrades which later were found to have cost around R250 million. Complaints were later made to the Public Protector who instituted an investigation into the misuse of state funds and found that allegations of the President unfairly benefitting from these upgrades were true. Reports by the Special Investigating Unit estimated that the upgrades to Nkandla cost more than 10 times what they should have.

2012

Protests increased dramatically in 2012, largely against lack of service delivery by government. The mining industry also saw a steep rise in industrial protest.

On 10 August, 3000 miners walked off a Lonmin-owned mine near Rustenberg in protest against failure of management to meet with them. This led to the most violent, single incident in the post-democratic period, when **44 people lost their lives in action resulting from a wildcat strike in Marikana.** Two police members and two private security guards were among the 10 people killed in the intimidation phase on 10 and 11 August, and a further 34 deaths and nearly 80 injuries occurred on 16 August when police opened fire on striking miners. The incident has become known as the **Marikana Massacre.**

President Jacob Zuma asked former Supreme Court of Appeals **Judge Ian Gordon Farlam** to lead a **commission of enquiry** into the massacre to uncover and find solutions to the challenges that led to this incident. This enquiry should clarify the roles of the National Union of Mine Workers (NUM), ACMU, the Lonmin management, the police and private security companies and the miners themselves.

By October it was estimated that more than 75 000 miners were on strike at various mines across the country. Most of these strikes were illegal, permission for the protests not having been obtained from the relevant authorities.

During 2012 **Julius Malema was suspended and then expelled** from the ANC as a result of convictions for hate speech and sowing divisions within the party. He courted controversy by encouraging the singing of 'Kill the farmer' songs at rallies and by praising the Zimbabwean President Robert Mugabe, as well as expressing controversial opinions about the ANC leadership and President Zuma in particular. Malema later faced charges of money laundering, racketeering and fraud related to his relationships with the government in the North West, and also non-payment of income tax. His personal home in Sandton, Johannesburg, was sold, as were several of his other properties and disposable assets.

With the growth and development of the **astronomical community**, South Africa has come to be favoured for its clear conditions, open spaces without light pollution and suitability for large telescope use. The **Square Kilometre Array** project will be split over South Africa, Australia and New Zealand and will join the South African Large Telescope (SALT) in the Karroo, the largest optical telescope in the southern hemisphere.

CIVIL SOCIETY

Many activists operated through non-profit, community-orientated organisations or religious bodies which contributed to the move to democracy. Civil society organisations are still strong, and those that concentrate on human rights or justice issues are not popular with government, although not under threat as they were under apartheid.

On the positive side, those working for NGOs are no longer harassed, offices are not raided by security police, leadership is not arrested and funding from overseas is allowed, although it has diminished due to the international economic decline. A lack of funding has led to the closure of many civil society organisations, such as the Institute for Democracy in South Africa (IDASA), which was liquidated in 2013.

The government, through the Department of Social Development, works with civil society in an attempt to regulate and control the administrations, but inefficiency and lack of communication has been prevalent with a lack of support most common.

One of the big issues addressed by civil society during this period was the promulgation of the Protection of State Information Bill, which aimed to control the leaking, circulation and publication of restricted information. The media sector in particular was concerned about the impact on accountability and transparency. Despite the formulation of a broad campaign (known as the Right to Know campaign, comprising over 200 organisations), a somewhat diluted form of the Bill was passed during 2013 and signed into law in early 2014.

2013

The **Economic Freedom Fighters** (EFF) party was formed as a result of efforts by ousted ANC member Julius Malema. Malema and 24 members of the EFF were elected to parliament in the 2014 national elections, and he was dismissed on 19 June following remarks blaming the government for the murder of 42 miners in Marikana in August 2012. EFF members of parliament have party distinguished themselves from the ANC by wearing red overalls and work clothes, and red berets to parliament.

On Valentine's day, the country awoke to the shocking news that South African Olympic athlete, **Oscar Pistorius,** had shot dead his girlfriend **Reeva Steenkamp** in his house in Pretoria East. The shooting drew unprecedented international attention due largely to Pistorius's reputation as a paralympian who ran on prosthetic legs. The trial in 2014 lasted many months and received coverage on a dedicated TV channel.

On 5 December, **Nelson Mandela,** aged 92, **died** at home after many months of illness and periods of hospitalisation. His wife, Graca Machel, was at his side during his illness both during his hospital periods and at home. He was discharged from hospital in September, and nursed at home until his death three months later. President Zuma announced a ten-day national mourning period, which included a lying-in-state, national days of prayer and reflection and the funeral. Ninety representatives of foreign states visited his home in Qunu to attend his funeral and memorial services.

2014

Twenty years after the first democratic elections many South Africans began returning to the country after having emigrated prior to the 2008 international financial crisis. It was estimated that over 350 000 people with highly sought-after skills returned during this year, slowing the steady outflow of mainly white South Africans during the first two decades of democracy.

EDUCATION IN SOUTH AFRICA

Major reform of the education system was necessary to move away from the 'Bantu Education' policies of the previous dispensation. In some ways this has been successful with schools now more integrated, but, according to a 2013 report, around 50 per cent of learners who start school never reach matriculation level.

Twenty years after democracy there is still a lack of facilities at many schools, no toilets or running water, inadequate classrooms and poor teaching, no sports facilities and, in some cases, no delivery of textbooks.

CHAPTER 12: THE SECOND POST-DEMOCRACY DECADE

The **Nkandla controversy** continued to plague the President even after the elections, with the 447-page report of the Public Protector clearly stating that he was aware of the scope of the renovations, some of which had little or nothing to do with security.

South African swimmers **Cameron van der Burgh and Chad le Clos** repeated their 2012 Olympic successes and won gold medals at the Commonwealth Games in the 50 metres breaststroke and 100 metres butterfly respectively.

National and provincial elections

The 20-year post-democracy National Elections, held in April 2014 were contested by more than 30 parties, with the ANC gaining the majority of 62.15 per cent (249 seats), a slight reduction on their previous majority. The Democratic Alliance improved their share to 22.23 per cent (89 seats) and the new Economic Freedom Front gained 6.35 per cent (25 seats) of the vote, exceeding the expectations of most political analysts. All other parties achieved a less than 2.5 per cent share, including the newly formed AGANG party, led by the academic and partner of the late Steve Biko, Mamphele Ramphela.

In the provincial results, the ANC held all but one of the provinces, with the Democratic Alliance again winning the Western Cape with an increased majority, and substantially increasing their share of votes in Gauteng.

Financial situation

In a rather depressing scenario of declining values of the South African Rand against the major world currencies, the increase in petrol and energy prices and other financial challenges, it is good to look at some positive developments in respect to various economic factors:

1. The South African stock market has achieved excellent results over the past decade showing little indication of the political challenges of the sub-continent and the economic challenges of the rest of the world.
2. The collection of income taxes has improved, ensuring a continued supply of money to support the grants system for children, the disabled and the elderly.

3. The Development Policy Research Unit at the University of Cape Town has published a paper on non-income welfare, measuring the delivery of public assets to the poor between 1993 and 2011. The measures included dwelling types, roof material, sources of drinking water, energy and sanitation. It was found that deprivation levels of the poor declined over the period, with a larger improvement between 1993 and 1998 compared with later periods. Levels of poverty in post-apartheid South Africa have declined continuously between 1993 and 2011, with African and female-headed households benefiting more than other groups.

Reopening of land claims

The land claims process was re-opened for the filing of additional claims (previously, no claim submitted after 31 December 1998 was considered for settlement or restitution). There were suggestions that claims pre-dating the 1913 Land Act would also be considered for the first time, creating the possibility of large-scale claims by South Africa's 'First People', the Khoi/San, but this did not appear in the legislation.

Several radical suggestions for the redistribution of farm land were also made, possibly in response to the popularity of the EFF, but at the time of publishing, none of these have been legislated.

Twenty years of democracy

As South Africans celebrated the twentieth anniversary of the first democratic elections in the country, the state took the opportunity to showcase achievements made during that time. Many of the statistics have been questioned by civil society analysts, but there is no doubt that service delivery has been extended and the provision of social grants has been a lifeline to the most vulnerable, albeit not at the rate which was envisioned during the apartheid era, or which has been promised to the electorate. State-issued statistics on the achievements made during 1994-2014 include:

- Sanitation: from 50 per cent of households in 1994/1995, to 83 per cent of households in 2011/2012.
- Water: from 60 per cent of households in 1994/1995, to over 95 per cent of households in 2011/2012.

- Electricity: from around 50 per cent of households in 1994/1995, to 86 per cent of households in 2011/2012.
- Life expectancy: The average life expectancy of South Africans improved from 51.6 years in 2005 to 59.6 in 2013.
- The proportion of people living in formal housing increased from 64 per cent in 1996 to 77.7 per cent in 2011

(Statistics above taken from 'Twenty year review 1994-2014' issued by the Office of the Presidency.

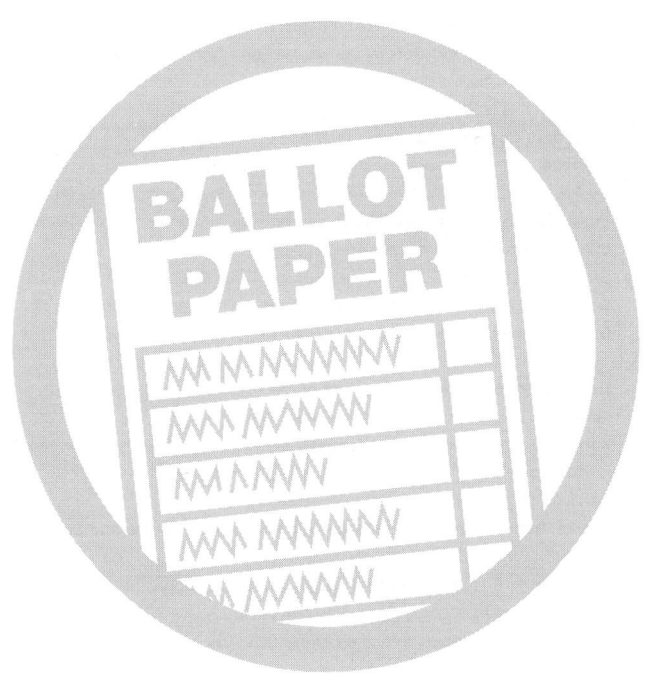

References and Recommended Reading

Alagiah, George: *A Passage to Africa*, 2001

Alexander, Neville: *Robben Island Dossier*, Rondebosch 1994

Barnard, F: *Thirteen Years in the Shadow of Dr H F Verwoerd*, Cape Town 1967

Bernstein, Hilda: *The World that Was Ours*, London 1989

Boonzaier, E et al: *The Cape Herders, Cape Town & Johannesburg*, David Philip and Ahtens: Ohio University Press 1996

Boraine, Alex: *On the Way to a Failed State*, South Africa 2014.

Botha, J: *Verwoerd is Dead*, Cape Town 1967

Brookes, Edgar & Webb, Colin: *A History of Natal,* Pietermaritzburg, 1965

Cameron, Trewhella and Spies, S.P. (eds): *An Illustrated History of South Africa*, Jonathan Ball Publishers 1986

Davenport, T R H: *South Africa: A Modern History*, London 1991

de Kock, Eugene and Gordin, Jeremy: *A Long Night's Damage: Working for the Apartheid State*, Saxonwold, SA 1998

De Villiers, H H W: Rivonia, *Operation Mayibuye*, Johannesburg 1964

Desmond, Cosmos: *The Discarded People,*

Dingake, M: *My fight against Apartheid*, London 1987

Du Preez, Max: *Pale Native: memories of a renegade reporter*, Cape Town, Zebra 2003

Edwards, Ian and Babenia, Natoo: *Memoirs of a Saboteur*, Cape Town 1995

Ellisannesburg, S: *Comrades Against Apartheid*, 1965

Ginsberg, Anthony: *South Africa's Future: From Crisis to Prosperity*, London 1998

Goldstuck, Arthur: *Ink in the Porridge and the Aardvark and the Caravan*, London 1994, 1999

Graaf, Michael: Hawks and Doves: *The Pro- and Anti-Conscription Press in South Africa*, Durban 1988

Holland, H: *The Struggle: A History of the ANC,* London 1989

Jenkin, T: *Escape from Pretoria*, London 1987

Karis, T: From Protest to Challenge: *A Documentary History of African Politics in South Africa,* Stanford 1973

Karis, T: *The Treason Trial in South Africa,* London 1958

Kasrils, Ronnie: *Armed and Dangerous: My undercover struggle against Apartheid*, London 1993

Lekota, M P: *Prison Letters to a Daughter*, Johannesburg 1991

Lings, Kevin: *The Missing Piece.* Pan Macmillan, South Africa 2014

MacLennan, Ben: *Apartheid, the Lighter Side*, Chameleon Press and Carrefour Press, Cape Town 1990

MacLennan, Ben: *The Wind Makes Dust: Four centuries of travel in South Africa*, Cape Town, Tafelberg 2003

Malan, Rian: *My Traitor's Heart*, London 1990

Mandela, Nelson Rolihlahla: *Long Walk to Freedom*, London, Abacus 1995

Mandela, Nelson Rolihlahla: *No Easy Walk to Freedom*, London 1965

Mandela, Nelson Rolihlahla: *The Struggle is My Life*, London 1986

Mason, David: *South Africa: A Traveller's History*, London, Phoenix/Windrush 2003

Mbeki, Govan: *Learning from Robben Island*, Cape Town 1991

Mbeki, Govan: *South Africa: The Peasants Revolt*, London 1964

Meer, Fatima: *Higher than Hope: Mandela*, Durban 1988

Meer, Fatima: *The Trial of Andrew Zondo*, Braamfontein 1987

Mountain, Alan: *The First People of the Cape*, Cape Town, David Philip 2003

Mtolo, B: *Umkhonto we Sizwe: The Road to the Left*, Durban 1966

Mtolo: *Umkhonto we Sizwe*

Nuttall, Tim et al: *From Apartheid to Democracy – South Africa 1948–1994*, Pietermaritzburg, Shuter and Shooter 1998

Pike, H: *A History of Communism in South Africa*, Germiston 1985

Sachs, Albie: *The Jail Diary*, Cape Town 1990

Sachs, Albie: *Running to Maputo*, London 1990

Sachs, B: *The Road from Sharpeville*, B New York 1961

Schoeman, Ben: *My lewe in die Politiek*, Johannesburg 1978

Smith, Charlene: *Robben Island*, Cape Town, Struik 1997

Sparks, Alistair: *Tomorrow is Another Country*,

Spink, Kathryn: *Black Sash: the Beginning of a Bridge in South Africa*, London 1991

Strydom, L: *Rivonia Unmasked*, Johannesburg?

Tambo, Oliver: *Preparing for Power: Olive Tambo Speaks*, Oxford 1987

Thom, H B: *D F Malan*, Cape Town 1980

Truth and Reconciliation Commission of South Africa: *Final Report*, TRC 1998

Twala, M and Bernard, E: *A Soldier's Story*, Johannesburg 1994 Mbokodo. Inside MK Mwezi Tgwala –

Welsh, Frank: *A History of South Africa*, London, Harper Collins 2000

Wilson, Daphne: *From Tribulation to Triumphs*, Cape Town 2002

Miscellaneous publications

The Mercury: *The 20th Century in Decades*

S A Family Encyclopaedia: *Peter Joyce*, Cape Town 1989

Survey of Race Relations: *S A Institute of Race Relations – various years*

List of Museums

There are over 300 museums in South Africa. This is a small selection to whet your appetite. For details of more museums, sorted by province, visit www.museums.org.za

AFRICAN WINDOW MUSEUM aka NATIONAL CULTURAL HISTORY MUSEUM
Tel: 012 324 6082

ALBANY MUSEUM COMPLEX, Grahamstown Tel: 046 622 3241; e-mail: info@grahamstown.co.za

ANTHROPOLOGY AND ARCHAEOLOGY, University of South Africa Tel: 012 429 3011; www.unisa.ac.za/dept/vir/mmuseum.html

ANTON VAN WOUW, Art, History, Culture Tel: 012 460 7422

APARTHEID MUSEUM, Johannesburg

BARTOLOMEU DIAS MUSEUM COMPLEX, Mossel Bay Tel: 044 691 1067;
e-mail: diasmuseum.mweb.co.za

BO KAAP MUSEUM, Cape Town Tel: 021 426 4260; e-mail: info@capetown.org

BUSHMEN'S CAVE MUSEUM, Giant's Castle Reserve, Drakensberg Tel: 036 353 3718;

CASTLE OF GOOD HOPE MILITARY MUSEUM, Cape Town Tel: 021 469 1249;
e-mail: casteel@cis.co.za

DISTRICT SIX MUSEUM, Cape Town Tel: 021 461 4735; e-mail: info@disrictsix.co.za

EAST LONDON MUSEUM, East London Tel: 043 722 6015; e-mail: eltour@mweb.co.za

EDOARDO VILLA MUSEUM Tel: 012 420 4017; email: villa@postino.up.ac.za

FORT DURNFORD MUSEUM, Estcourt, KZN

FORT KLAPPERKOP Pretoria Tel: 012 460 3235

GREYTOWN MUSEUM, Greytown, KZN Tel: 033 413 1171

GROOT CONSTANTIA WINE MUSEUM, Western Cape Tel: 021 794 5128;
e-mail: gct@mweb.co.za

JAMES HALL MUSEUM OF TRANSPORT, Johannesburg Tel: 011 435 9718

JAN SMUTS HOUSE, Doornkloof Farm, Irene Tel: 012 667 1176

JLB SMITH INSTITUTE, Grahamstown Tel: 046 336 1002

KILLIE CAMPBELL MUSEUM, Durban Tel: 031 209 5066

KIMBERLEY MINE MUSEUM, Kimberley

KOOPMANS-DE WET HOUSE, Cape Town Tel: 021 424 2473

KRUGER HOUSE MUSEUM, Pretoria Tel: 012 326 9172

MELROSE HOUSE, Pretoria Tel: 012 322 2805; e-mail: melrosehouse@intekom.co.za

MISSION HOUSE MUSEUM, Hermannsburg, KZN Tel: 033 445 0405

MUSEUM AFRICA, Johannesburg Tel: 011 833 5624; e-mail: museum@mj.org.za

NATAL MARITIME MUSEUM, Durban Tel: 031 300 6324

NATIONAL MUSEUM, Bloemfontein Tel: 051 447 9609

OWL HOUSE, Nieu Bethesda, Free State Tel: 049 841 1659; e-mail: owlhouse@intekom.co.za

PIERNEEF MUSEUM, Pretoria Tel: 012 323 1419

PIONEER MUSEUM Pioneer dwelling (c.1848) Silverton, Pretoria Tel: 012 803 6086

PRETORIA ART MUSEUM, Pretoria Tel: 012 344 1807; e-mail: artmuseumpta@intekom.co.za

ROBBEN ISLAND MUSEUM, 11 km north of Cape Town Tel: 021 419 1300:
    e-mail: bookings@robben-island.org.za

RUST EN VREUGD, Cape Town Tel: 021 465 3628

S A JEWISH MUSEUM. Cape Town Tel: 012 445 1546; www.sajewishmuseum.co.za

SAMMY MARKS MUSEUM, Pretoria Tel: 012 803 6158

SOUTH AFRICAN AIRFORCE MUSEUM, Cape Town Tel: 021 508 6377; www.saafmuseum.co.za

SOUTH AFRICAN AIRFORCE MUSEUM, Port Elizabeth Tel: 041 505 1295; www.saafmuseum.co.za

SOUTH AFRICAN AIRFORCE MUSEUM, Pretoria Tel: 012 351 2153; www.saafmuseum.co.za

SOUTH AFRICAN MUSEUM AND PLANETARIUM, Cape Town Tel: 021 424 3330;
    e-mail: tferreira@samuseum.ac.za

SOUTH AFRICAN NATIONAL GALLERY, Cape Town Tel: 021 465 1628

STELLENBOSCH VILLAGE MUSEUM, Stellenbosch Tel: 021 887 2902;
    e-mail: stelmus@mweb.co.za

TALANA MUSEUM, Dundee, KZN

TRANSVAAL MUSEUM, Pretoria Tel: 012 322 7632; www.nfi.co.za

TSWAING CRATER MUSEUM, Pretoria Tel: 012 790 2302

VOORTREKKER MONUMENT MUSEUM, Pretoria Tel: 012 323 0682

VOORTREKKER MUSEUM, Pietermaritzburg, KZN Tel: 033 394 6834
    www.voortrekkermuseum.co.za

WILLEM PRINSLOO AGRICULTURAL MUSEUM, Pretoria Tel: 012 734 171

Index